Gullies of My People

The University of Georgia Press *Athens*

Gullies of My People

An Excavation of Landscape and Family

JOHN LANE

*Publication of this work was made
possible, in part, by a generous gift from
the University of Georgia Press Friends Fund.*

Library of Congress Control Number: 2023937189
ISBN: 9780820365442 (paperback)
ISBN: 9780820365459 (epub)
ISBN: 9780820365466 (PDF)

Title page spread image: Active Roadside Gully Formed
in an Old Roadbed near Switzer, S.C., March 1935, Soil
Conservation Service (Photo from the South Caroliniana
Library, University of South Carolina, Columbia, S.C.)

p. vi and part openers: From *Principles of Gully Erosion
in the Piedmont of South Carolina,* by H. A. Ireland,
C. F. Sharpe, and D. H. Eargle (Washington, D.C.:
U.S. Department of Agriculture, 1939)

For Sandy

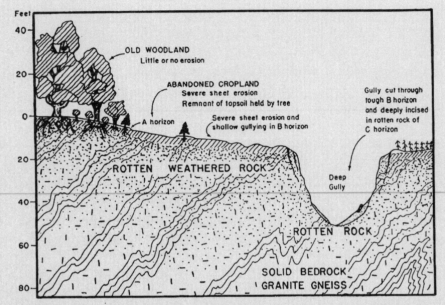

FIGURE 7.—Relation of sheet erosion and gullying to soil horizons, zone of weathering, and solid bedrock. The deep gully can cut downward 5 to 8 feet more before reaching solid bedrock, where its progress will be checked.

The southern story is not one into which it is possible to jump rapidly because things are not always what they seem.

GEOGRAPHER CARL O. SAUER,
Spartanburg, South Carolina, June 30, 1936

Contents

Breaking Ground: My Past as a Gully   1

A. HORIZON

    Big Lots Gully   13

    Deep Family History   23

    Marshall Tucker Gully   37

    Chinquapins   43

    Restoration   49

B. HORIZON

    Cox Gully   57

    Beauty Queen   61

    Legacy   67

    Irwin Avenue   75

C. HORIZON

    Rediscovering the Bradleys   85

    Sandy Ground   93

    Slump   101

    Downtown Gullies   109

    Enoree Flume   123

BEDROCK

Briarcliff Road   141

Alverson Gully   151

This Book Belongs to Mary Lane   167

Airport Gully   181

Furrows in Mama's Backyard   187

TAILINGS

A Genealogy: Mama's Side   195

Acknowledgments   197

Source Notes   199

Bio   203

Gullies of My People

Mama and Sister on the Edge (Photographer Unknown, 1944)

Breaking Ground   *My Past as a Gully*

Escaping the house was one of my earliest forms of therapy. Motion proved to be a geographical self-medication. Once I discovered my love for the outdoors, that love saved me. There was plenty of trouble in my immediate family, and I often needed to escape. Spartanburg is a mid-sized South Carolina city in the upper Piedmont, a region of low-rolling hills and flashy streams. The physiographic province extends between the mountains and ocean from New York to Alabama, and, even though it is urbanized and suburbanized in many areas, the landscape still offers plenty of grown-over and neglected spaces that offer opportunities to slip away.

As a child I didn't call it the Piedmont. That name would come later when I understood the physical world enough to know how it's organized and studied by earth scientists based on surface topography and underlying geology. I find great satisfaction in reviewing the forces that made the land, the patterns, and the processes. What has mattered always is getting out into the fields and woods and not letting my home life cave in and cover me.

I discovered Dead Horse Canyon in my neighborhood wanderings, and years later I learned how the place got its name: as a bone yard for local livestock, carcasses hauled in from pastures to rot in the gully. By the time I discovered my way there, Dead Horse Canyon was just a name. The flesh fed generations of buzzards, and the bones were gnawed to dust by wild dogs and mice.

Whatever else Dead Horse Canyon was, that magic depression, that shady retreat in the hard level earth, red from near the surface downward, was an open door into the landscape. I routinely wandered out and ran across a pasture that today is lined with houses. I entered the distant hardwoods and acres of bamboo, and somewhere beyond that gully portal, I always found sanctuary.

1

Dead Horse Canyon deepened to the south; north, toward the gully's head, a plunge pool waited, dry except after rains that would extend its upper limits, for a gully is a living thing, responding to rain and time. A gully, like me, is the child of flow. Water is a buzz saw. At the end where Dead Horse Canyon was open and deepest, it was two or three times as tall as me. The flat floor intersected with a creek, and that creek in turn intersected with a larger creek. The sky above, blue or cloudy by the day, was widest at the intersection as well. All along the gully opened out a broad debris field, a junkyard, where ancient cars and appliances had been pushed over the gully's rim and tumbled down, where for years and maybe even decades, they had rusted among the small pines and rabbit tobacco that grew up seasonally on the flat gully bottom. Chrome auto bumpers gleamed with mica flecks. A primary use of local gullies is to find low places and fill them up, a common disposal practice in the region since settlement.

Now that I know the tripartite rules of erosion, transportation, and deposition, how fluvial motion creates topography and opens wounds, I see everything as mixed up and in flux. What is stable is sent packing. The moment a gully begins is like trauma to a plowed field. All around me in the Piedmont, eroded soil, raw fields, are often set in motion by downpours, destroying coherence. I loved the way a gully surrounded me and hugged me close, gave me protection, armored me against the chaos of my life. I sat for many hours in that deep gully shade.

Out West, gullies are mostly called canyons, but they're also called arroyos and gulches; the French call them defiles and couloirs. There are many names for gullies, but they are always a trench cut into the land by the action of running water. Gully is an old English word for alley, those places off the main drag, the stitches tying together proper streets. And alley isn't far removed from ally, the support needed for my collapsing world of childhood. In cultural terms, gullies are wounds that never heal. Kudzu covers them; people hide or dispose of things in them; after decades, the hidden becomes visible only to the practiced eye. I'd always been drawn to these wounds that never stop bleeding, where red clay flows after rains and dry scabs are left after long periods of erosion.

If I left our house on Washington Road and ran the other direction away from the gully, I could follow the asphalt to town just like the school bus traveled most weekdays from September to June. I preferred exploring Dead Horse Canyon rather than going to school or town, and that might be one of the reasons I was held back in first grade. There were other reasons too. My mother was often drunk back then, and she didn't keep close tabs on me. My sister Sandy, in her middle teens, had already taken a job at a drugstore downtown, but she was still my bedrock. She checked on me and made sure I was fed. In spite of Sandy's oversight, I was still free to create my own path to self-reliance.

When I started school, it wasn't uncommon for me to forge Mama's signature on report cards, which were often mediocre and occasionally bottom-of-the-barrel bad. I somehow survived, though, and later even flourished emotionally and intellectually. They say some mountain ranges make their own weather and for my sister and me it was like that. There was little oxygen in our depleted household, and so whatever care and assistance we had we often made for each other.

After Daddy committed suicide, we stayed awhile in Southern Pines, a resort town in the sandhills at the edge of the North Carolina coastal plain. I possess a few memories of those years in Southern Pines, but I am sure that had I stayed in that place, I would have grown to love the longleaf pines and residual dune lines left after the Miocene seas advanced and retreated millions of years before.

Sandy has told me that some time after Daddy died, I took off on my own. I headed across town to visit an aunt and cousins. I was five years old when I knocked on their front door. I'd crossed several big roads and the main line of the railroad to get there. What was I running from as a child? Daddy was dead and Mama was already struggling with alcoholism, but no one at home hit me. I had regular meals. When Mama returned to Spartanburg, we entered a large, extended family, including aunts, uncles, and cousins. Even as a child I understood that not just landscapes were subject to larger forces. By 1962 my family had been gullied for decades, likely for centuries.

Mama died in 2004. By that time she'd been sober for twenty years. She might ask me from beyond the grave why I am now making so much of the gullies of my childhood. Everything turned out all right, she might remind me—I'm well educated, had a long career as a professor, have a happy marriage, have a nice house. "I was the one with the hard life," she might observe, "not you."

Yet I might remind her that this story belongs not just to her, but also to the whole family. There's no way to separate a gully from its tributaries. The life we led was enough to erode anyone's sense of self. It surely shaped me. By 1962, when we moved to Washington Road, I was just beginning to find my way to some sense of what might be called equilibrium, but Mama wasn't quite there yet. For many years yet to come she carried Sandy and me along like stream-rounded pebbles in a flash flood. We lived in eleven houses in ten years.

Accelerate time forward from that gully-loving boy, and I'd bumble through chemistry and biology but fall in love with geology in college, having discovered an evangelist for rocks, landscapes, and time, a master teacher named John Harrington who sharpened my eye to, as Blake advised, "see the world in a grain of sand," or better yet, to see the world in the bottom of a gully.

As a geology student in college my teacher taught me "the Wasness of the Is." I learned to see that "the Now is a window into the Then." I learned that one of the best ways to read the past is to look for scars on the land, places where the earth has been peeled away by water, wind, or mechanical action, revealing the land's layered history. Why not a human life as well?

By the early 1800s the southern Piedmont had been battered and scarred by human use. Soil erosion and the decline in soil fertility had already caught the attention of geologists. In the 1840s British geologist Charles Lyell toured the South and commented on the gullying. He saw the Piedmont's already extensive gullies as a record of erosion and the way humans could transform landscapes. By the 1900s the severe erosion of Piedmont farmland astonished scientists who were beginning to study it.

By the 1930s the effects of erosion highlighted by drought and dust storms on the Great Plains exacerbated the need for research and understanding. Gullying affected more than half the land in the Piedmont, and one of the most severely gullied landscapes in the country was the southern Piedmont.

Cotton farming was one of the main culprits. The crop monopolized production by small upland farmers, who, through ignorance or poverty, used poor farming practices; inattention contributed to the ruin of their cropland. The farmers, always on the edge of poverty and at the whim of the weather, spiraled deeper into despair as the gullies formed. The topsoil washed off the land—as much as four to eighteen inches all over the Piedmont. As the upper layers of soil washed into the numerous streams downslope, the erosion exposed the bright orange and red clay that the Piedmont is known for today.

In the depth of the Great Depression, in August 1933, the Soil Erosion Service (SES) was established in the Department of Interior with the intent of battling soil erosion nationwide. Later, in 1935, the service was transferred to the United States Department of Agriculture and became the Soil Conservation Service (SCS). The gullies in the southern half of the Piedmont, in Spartanburg County, South Carolina, were huge. The SCS set up its southeastern headquarters in Spartanburg and dispatched agents in all directions to work with the impoverished farmers. These agents taught the farmers better farming practices such as terracing, and they provided instruction on crop rotation and the repair of gullied land. The Service also brought in a platoon of earth scientists who set up research projects concerning the soil and geology of the Piedmont region.

In 2015 Terry Ferguson, a local earth scientist, visited the Spartanburg County Library to look at some old photos of the Soil Conservation Service that were archived in a scrapbook. The scrapbook, what many scientists might consider an inconsequential informal publication, languished for eighty years in the files of the local historical society, but Terry's review uncovered information that he had never seen before.

Terry is a good friend. He often functions as a bemused guide, particularly in the zones where science and personal reflection intersect. Terry serves the purpose of sounding board for my deepest inquiries into time and space. He tolerates my questions and doesn't offer easy answers. Ours is a friendship open to sudden reflective phone calls and endless tailgate discussion.

There had been a classic geology monograph, *Principles of Gully Erosion*, published in 1939 by D. H. "Hoye" Eargle and two other Soil Conservation Service scientists, H. A. Ireland and S. F. S. Sharpe. Terry was familiar with the work, so he knew that much of the research had been done in Spartanburg County. He wondered, what else could be in the historical society files? The gully monograph deals with a series of research sites, but in the scrapbook, Terry located other information about research that had not been included in *Principles of Gully Erosion*.

Going through the scrapbook, Terry found something unexpected and exciting: the photos showed "buried organic deposits." These photos were exciting because they revealed features that geologists did not expect to find in the Piedmont such as buried valleys, the bottoms of which contained thick deposits of organic material that looked like coal seams. The deposits seen in the photos and articles were at least a hundred thousand years old, and consisted of beetles, tree trunks, branches, beaver sticks, leaves, seeds, mats of moss, sedges, grasses, peat, all rich in pollen. The dark deposits had been softened and disintegrated with time, then been compressed and entombed. Some of the trees were charred by fire. On the black-and-white photos they looked dark brown, but *in situ* they are gray-black and shine, as the soil researchers claimed, "with a resinous luster." To Terry, they were as exciting as fossil dinosaurs. At some point I knew he would ask me to ponder the presence and meaning of those mysterious buried organic deposits of the Pleistocene that were discovered in the 1930s, or as Terry put it, "discovered, forgotten, discovered, and forgotten again."

As Terry dug deeper into the 1930s research of the Soil Conservation Service, he discovered forgotten documents, field notes, and other obscure publications in the National Agricultural Library and the National Archives, much of it by Hoye Eargle, a South Carolina native, who became one of the key Depression-era "ghost researchers" Terry soon was chasing. With the intellectual freedom weirdly granted by the Great Depression, Eargle looked beyond the fairly recent agricultural development of gullies into the development of the Piedmont landscape as a whole. From his colleagues' observations, Eargle hypothesized that the Piedmont landscape may have been formed differently than contemporary geologists in the 1930s thought. The prevailing science at that time (still prevailing today) presented the idea that the Piedmont as a physiographic region was stable and that its soils were mostly formed gradually from in-place weathering of bedrock. But Eargle discovered ancient buried valleys in Spartanburg County's upland areas that didn't fit with this view. This meant that a high percentage of the soils in the Piedmont had actually been transported to fill in these ancient valleys. "If Eargle had not been studying the historic gullies in Spartanburg County, he would not have found the buried organic deposits," Terry explained. "When he found them, he wondered, 'Whoa! Where did this stuff come from?'"

How was all of Eargle's research forgotten for so long? The amount of fieldwork he did in five years in Spartanburg County was extraordinary. He explored many sites extensively, and Terry believed Eargle and his team of Roosevelt's CCC workers had hand-augered upward of a thousand bore holes to compile their data. How did all of this disappear into obscurity?

Terry says I should be careful; claiming complete obscurity for Hoye Eargle's ideas is a vast simplification. Several contemporary geologists are aware of some of this work because the monograph *Principles of Gully Erosion* has remained an important and widely quoted work in the soil conservation field. However, none of Eargle's results on the buried valleys or the buried organic deposits were published except for a brief 1940 article in the journal *Science*. World War II brought Eargle's Piedmont research to a halt in 1942 when his division ceased to exist and he went on to work for the U.S. Geological Survey. Eargle did go on to write a master's thesis using some of his research on gullies, but it was never published. He never finished his doctorate. Because of these circumstances, Eargle's ideas about the formation of the Piedmont were never in wide distribution and even now remain only a footnote at best. A friend in a memorial remembered Eargle as "a walking encyclopedia for the lands he knew."

Listening to Terry I got the feeling that he knows he's stumbled, late in his career, onto data and fieldwork that will be important and compelling to the present and future community of geologists and soil scientists. The ghost of Hoye Eargle had led the way.

After Terry's discovery in the library and subsequent field confirmation, he asked me to drive a van for a weekend geology field trip for several dozen people. Later, I became his research assistant on a series of visits to other gullies in Upstate South Carolina, mostly in Spartanburg County. That first field trip took place in 2017, and then over four years I took a number of additional outings with him and his earth scientist colleagues. I didn't know when I started working with Terry that hidden in the gullies we'd explore were the dark residual landscapes of the long-ago Piedmont that had been discovered by those soil scientists of the Soil Conservation Service working in Spartanburg County in the 1930s, or that in these organic-rich deposits I'd find great comfort and see them as metaphors for my own interior life. Because I am digging down with my words, I call the process of drafting this book "excavations." That's what it felt like as I began to compile my notes from all my excursions.

It is obvious that I believe that the Piedmont's geological landscape and our family landscape overlap, and that I believe they cannot be separated. If I have a thesis, it is that. My genetic material has been circulating in the Piedmont for a long time. My people have been here for over ten generations, and we are often overlooked and underestimated, even scorned. Reviewing our story reveals personal revelations and accommodations and creates an outline of who I am and where I came from, not only genetically but also intellectually and geographically.

I have lived with the consequences—genetics, choices, and actions forced upon us by consequences and history—of many generations of southern ancestors. One way to look at the body is as a cleared field, plowed and gullied over time. Gullies can start and stop in a day. They can be corrected, filled in, redirected, played in, studied, or ignored.

At the time I began to go into the field with Terry to explore the gullies of Spartanburg County, I had my thesis confirmed by taking road trips with my sister Sandy to visit sites and landscapes associated with our family—vanished and standing houses, farms, graveyards, textile mills. What I discovered as I examined our family's past was that I was mapping my own interior as well. Inside and outside of me were Piedmont back roads and brambles, winding gullies, old farmland, dark streams, and ramshackle mill houses. Many of these places were pegged to difficult stories and telling those stories made them surface and even come alive.

Mama's family always curated a large number of stories refreshed by the telling. Over time, I have become aware that there are raw stories too, like ore before smelting, stories unknown or even unavailable to me. When I ask Sandy for those, they open up what I call gullies of feeling. The feelings flow around my own identity, and what survives of our southern family. Here I tell as much of the geology and our family's stories as I can, and I have assembled it all into horizons. As I auger through each layer, I discover more and more about my geological and personal Piedmont. As I have said, geology and identity cannot be separated in my mind.

As the crow flies, my old gully refuge called Dead Horse Canyon is only three miles from where I now live with my wife Betsy in an odd yet beautiful suburban house next to a creek. The transition from the childhood rental house to this neighborhood is an outward sign of the route my upwardly mobile life has taken. When I tap into my deep memories I follow to where the foot of that first gully once intersected with a flowing stream. If I trace the route myself, I enter my own terra incognita. In the interior space of memory, I locate the gully, I enter remembered space, and I note a change in temperature and bird song. I don't often recall the fear and emotional turmoil of childhood that sent me to the woods. I notice what is blooming because it's often summer in my memory, the season of most of my exploration as a child—cross vine, Japanese honeysuckle, Chinese privet. I find comfort in naming nature nearby, even if it is in naming a gully that's mostly in my memory.

So, I sit here and remember. As I have said, gullies seldom heal. At some point, people try to forget their injuries and move on, but there are usually scars, as there are scars on this abused land. We come to believe that there are clear running streams no matter how muddy the water once was. My soul is an etching, a relief drawing. In my imagination I fill in the gullied space. But under a thin layer of kudzu and leaf duff there are still signs of raw ditches, sluices. Betsy listens to me tell the stories of my family origins, often dark, and says, "Look at you. You have climbed out of many gullies by now."

My horizons are out the door. Dead Horse Canyon was long ago the center of my world, if a hole can have a center. Every walk as a child was a palimpsest, a page of my young life written over daily, then written over and over again. Now I will go back and venture into the old gullied woods of the Piedmont with Terry. I will visit the old family houses with my sister. I will scratch on that old page again.

A. Horizon

Often referred to as topsoil. This layer contains dark decomposed organic matter, which is called humus. It is most commonly described in terms relative to deeper layers.

OLD WOODLAND
Little or no erosion

ABANDONED CROPLAND
Severe sheet erosion
Remnant of topsoil held by tree

Severe sheet erosion and
shallow gullying in B horizon

A horizon

Gull
toug
and
in r
C h

ROTTEN WEATHERED ROCK

Deep
Gully

ROTTEN ROCK

SOLID BEDROCK
GRANITE GNEISS

Terry Ferguson Explaining Gully Dynamics (John Lane, 2017)

Big Lots Gully

On an unseasonably warm Saturday morning in February, The Friends of the Pleistocene field trip was off to a chaotic start. The Friends of the Pleistocene ("a non-organization organization") met once a year in every region of the United States. The Friends of the Pleistocene may be the only scientific gathering pledging friendship to a geologic epoch, and there was a high probability it was the only such group with its own official song ("We're friends of the Pleistocene; damn little ice we've seen . . .") sung to the tune of "Little Buttercup" by Gilbert and Sullivan.

Terry tried to coordinate the groggy, overeducated horde that had piled out into the parking lot of the Cedar Springs Shopping Center on the south side of Spartanburg.

"John, get a head count," he yelled in his field voice. "Count off if you have a head." My final count after several false starts and stops was "around sixty-two, probably with some error."

Among those present were sizable academic groups from Duke, University of Georgia, University of North Carolina–Charlotte, and University of South Carolina. Among the unaffiliated were citizen geologists, off-duty Department of Natural Resources agents, curious botanists, structural engineers, city planners, and graduate students, some showing signs of sleep deprivation after a campout at the nearby state park. Several folks had driven from as far away as Upstate New York and some, like me, came from within our nearby late Holocene home range. There were at least thirty undergraduates as well—many from UNCC, who were on a required field trip for two courses in their major.

Terry, the bespectacled college professor with the white beard, called again for order. I knew that he had a weakness for jokes, part data and part humor, and that his answers to direct questions are often sprinkled with "maybe" or "possibly." It is hard to get a straight-up "yes" from him, the world being a place always changing, always under scrutiny, and never fully understood. This is one reason we are friends. There is also in me a natural inclination to make a joke, but I do it to head off sadness and melancholy. When I was five Daddy's suicide placed me psychologically. I didn't worry so much about understanding as I did about stability. Daddy's absence made me acutely aware the world can change overnight. Everything can shift. Daddy lost his place in the world and I have always been determined to retain my balance—I do it by staying busy. Through the decades I have been father, lover, husband, teacher, poet, seeker, and that morning, on Terry's field trip, van driver.

Terry's academic bailiwick and profession is teacher and geo-archaeologist. He taught with me at nearby Wofford College for decades. When Terry arrived at Wofford as a freshman in 1971, he thought he wanted to major in psychology, but he quickly found out that the behaviorists were in power. "I wanted Jung and depth psychology," he once told me, "and I wasn't very interested in running rats." He tried physics, but after working on Native American rock shelters during a January term sponsored by our shared mentor John Harrington, he became interested in archaeology.

The young scholar discovered as an undergraduate that he loved research, and that he was good at it. The summer before his junior year he worked at an archaeological field school in New Mexico and used his nine hours credit to anchor a major in sociology. Even after he chose sociology, Terry's intellectual interests stayed broad, including upper-level English classes where he studied the high modernists, including James Joyce. "I've always been interested in the mind of man," Terry once said, "but I ended up looking at the mind of the earth."

For his master's thesis at the University of Tennessee, Terry wrote about soapstone quarries in northwestern South Carolina. His doctorate dissertation at Tennessee was on prehistoric settlement patterns on the Cumberland Plateau of Tennessee and Kentucky. When he landed back at Wofford in the mid-eighties, Terry continued John Harrington's tradition of teaching geology as a liberal art, though he never lost touch with his love of "depth" in any intellectual form. After Harrington retired, Terry reconstructed our old teacher's field labs, taught from his notes, curated his books and papers, even occupied his old office. The strong spirit of John Harrington stood behind everything Terry did for decades.

I beat the social odds and ended up at Wofford in the very same town where I'd grown up. Back then, Wofford was a private college, but through the connections of a guidance counselor who believed in me, I was provisionally accepted. I took geology—physical, historical, and regional problems—because I was on a search for something I couldn't find in English classes, and I thought maybe I could find that something in the study of rocks and time. Field geology as Harrington taught it offered a spark as to what I was searching for, and that spark was curiosity.

My freshman year in college I made eight Cs. I teetered on the verge of academic failure. Nothing had lit my fuse. Then I passed, in one college semester, from blind to seeing. The sweet grace of curiosity that followed is something that I summon in the hardest of times. It is a vehicle I still trust.

Harrington's courses had fostered in me a sense of impending change hanging over yards, blocks, cities, farm fields, even wood lots and hunt clubs. Mountains as tall as the Himalayas had once loomed over what would one day would be called Spartanburg. Along the muddy Piedmont creeks lived the distant cousins of plants the dinosaurs ate; giant volcanoes, now evident only in their erosion-exposed magma chambers, had once spewed ash within an easy drive of downtown. Over a foot of Piedmont topsoil built up over hundreds of thousands of years on the hilly landscape had been lost in only two hundred years, mostly on account of clear-cutting of the deep deciduous forests followed by bad farming practices. What was left was depleted Piedmont soils, diminished by erosion.

In my college years and beyond, I looked outward to the hills and streams for meaning as often as I looked within. Geology has been taught at Wofford since the nineteenth century when Warren Dupre took students on weeklong field trips. In the first decades of the twentieth century, geology dropped out of the curriculum for a time, and then picked up again in the 1950s. In 1964, John Harrington came to teach after a successful career as a geology professor at SMU and as a petroleum geologist and consultant working out of Chapel Hill. The story of Harrington's hiring was once legendary at Wofford and stands in humorous contrast to today's tedious search committees, campus visits, and "job talks." In the early 1960s the dean of the college, Philip Covington, met Harrington on a flight home to North Carolina. Covington sat in the window seat looking out. "What do you see down there, Lad?" John Harrington asked. Then Harrington spent the entire flight explaining the geology of the eastern United States to Covington based on what was passing below. Covington offered Harrington a job on the spot, and the next year he took it.

Calling himself "Professor Grope" for his view of science as sleuthing, Harrington taught mostly non-science majors like me from 1964 until 1981. In many ways, Harrington's three courses made up what today might be called a "program." His popular classes drew a tenth of the student body at one time. Students who studied with him learned to see the world broadly and across disciplines, or as his literary hero Sherlock Holmes advised, gather data, cultivate a critical eye, and go where the evidence leads. The goal was to learn to view nature and culture in a larger global context.

Harrington taught us that any Piedmont story begins in the basement of time. Harrington introduced us to what was becoming known as plate tectonics—crustal plates colliding, mountains rising, an ancestral ocean opening, mountains eroding, the present ocean basin closing and opening again. All this action, Harrington explained, happened at about the speed your fingernails grow, and yet over many millions of years, the Atlantic stretched and stretched to the width it holds now, vast and blue between the North American and Eurasian plates. The Atlantic basin was opening then, in the mid-seventies, and still is, though at some point in the deep future the plates will shift again, a plot turn in a play with no denouement, and Europe and Africa will again ride our way, closing the gap once more between here and there.

From central Alabama to the Hudson River, the Piedmont is the region lying west of the coastal plain and east of the Appalachian Mountains. At its widest in the Carolinas and Virginia, it is over a hundred miles of hilly expanse, a dissected peneplain, sloping gently to the Southeast. Stream erosion has gradually worn the mountains away. Nowhere is the original surface preserved. The Piedmont's boundary west of Spartanburg is at about nine hundred feet above sea level. The peaks, like White Oak Mountain to the West, rise to three thousand feet. The western boundary to the East is the Fall Zone, most easily perceived in the streams leaving the region to enter the coastal plain over a series falls and rapids. Below this Fall Zone, the hard rocks of the Piedmont lie beneath the sediments of the coastal plain.

Harrington called this "the dance of the continents." Because of his teaching we students saw massive mountains high as the Himalayas, and between Spartanburg and the opening Atlantic, we imagined ten miles of rock eroded in 250 million years.

Each Wednesday two Trailways busses rolled out to view road cuts, quarries, and streams. We saw stretches of Piedmont and Blue Ridge landscape we would have never visited if we had not been in the class. Many simply learned to appreciate basic geology and fulfilled their science requirement; a few were changed for life.

By my sophomore year at Wofford I was also seriously taking up the practice of poetry. What I remember about those early poems is that I was already interested in sound and images. In one poem I used the image "hewn stone wall," a long and two soft stresses. I like to think that my genetic assent to poetic craft could be tracked through that tiny speck of poetry DNA. I also like that stone is a part of it.

After college I boarded an airliner for a night flight from Atlanta to Seattle. From SeaTac, I hitchhiked to Port Townsend for what I thought would be a two-week visit—a week at the Festival of American Fiddle Tunes, and then a week at the Centrum Writers Conference. It was my first trip to the West. I didn't come back to the South for a year. The year I lived in the Pacific Northwest, one of my habitations was a little cabin right on the beach at Discovery Bay, connected to the Strait of Juan de Fuca on the Olympic Peninsula. That fall, from October until Christmas, I thought a great deal about landscape, sitting on the porch, looking out at the bay, and then to the Olympic Mountains beyond. I thought about the appeal of a new landscape but couldn't get past my nostalgia for the one I'd left behind. I wrote a letter to John Harrington that fall that became a poem; it says much more than I ever could about the juxtaposition of space and deep time. I began my long-ago poem, "To a Geologist," with the lines, "I've been reading Blake and thought / of you—'To see a World/in a grain of sand.' I know / what follows, Eternity, but for me,/here, time catches."

Besides teaching, Terry's professional work for forty years was focused on rocks, soils, and the points of contact between people and the landscape through time. Terry calls himself "a scientific generalist not a specialist," and as a generalist he knows a little about a lot of things and he thinks maybe more often than most specialists about relationships. There are disadvantages to Terry's generalist nature—he is perpetually underfunded, often distracted, and, because he taught at a small college rather than a large research university, somewhat isolated—he only acquired one student every four or five years who really showed interest and engagement in his geographical, geological, and sociological passions.

The Friends of the Pleistocene gathering was perfect for Terry to showcase his discovery of the wide-ranging research that was once conducted in Spartanburg County. Terry had recreated a portion of an April 1940 four-day field trip organized by Hoye Eargle for Soil Conservation Service researchers as a way to introduce their insights to a group of the nation's most prominent geologists, geographers, soil scientists, and ecologists. Terry had set up this Friends of the Pleistocene field trip to track the route of the long-forgotten Soil Conservation Service field trip seventy-nine years earlier where Hoye Eargle took twenty-nine scientists to view his study sites. The places Eargle and the others had visited in 1940 were at that time ongoing research sites where much work had already been done. On

Eargle's trip, the scientists pondered and questioned the discoveries with their colleagues, and Eargle produced a report that Terry found at the National Agricultural Library. No one knew at that time that the research would come to a screeching halt with the United States' entry into World War II in December 1941. Terry hoped he could rekindle the spirit of research in us.

"Open your field guide to stop #1," Terry yelled. "If you didn't print your field guide, I have brought along visual aids." He held up a large poster, a satellite photo of the very parking lot we were standing in.

"Right under your feet was a gully known as the Foster's Tavern Gully. It was called that by the Soil Conservation Service researchers in the 1930s because of that big house over there at that intersection." Like a weatherman with a screen behind him, Terry pointed to a Colonial-era tavern now looking quite threatened, pinched on all sides by fast food restaurants, drug stores, and a Walmart. "If we deployed ground penetrating radar and ran transects, we'd find evidence of the gully under this parking lot. In 1935 this was an active gully, but it's been filled for this shopping center. If you look at the parking lot, you can see places where the fill has settled."

I looked out at the cracked, wavy pavement of the parking lot. The old pavement was buckled and warped by time. Underneath, the ghost of the old gully had taken its toll. I knew the very ground we stood on was in motion. I imagined the parking lot was creeping toward the Big Lots, and the Big Lots, underlaid with soil, not rock, was inching downslope. The land literally wasn't where it was millions of years ago. Given enough geologic time, cataclysmic events would commence only a short distance from where you stood. Everything shifts in time. Everything is headed somewhere, usually downhill.

Soon enough my reverie was over and the Friends of the Pleistocene meeting itself was finally in motion. I piled in the van with a dozen participants, drove a hundred yards, and pulled in behind the shopping center. There was a set of soccer fields on one side, and it was obvious from the slope of the terrain that the cut from the fields was the source of the fill for the shopping center parking lot. I had a special affection for that late twentieth-century sports complex. In the summer of 1972, I was eighteen years old, and I spent many days walking transects on the newly graded front field with a wheelbarrow, picking up gravel for Spartanburg Parks & Recreation. The soccer field had been stable in its use for forty-five years, but things were not always what they seemed to be. Before the building of the shopping center and the sports complex, the field had been a gullied hillside, something akin to the ruined agricultural landscape that Terry would show us throughout the day. As I passed the field in the van, I flashed back to my role of clearing those fields as a teenager, one wheelbarrow at a time.

We soon parked, piled out, and headed into the woods. The sports complex was at our backs. We passed into the trees. The gully yawned before me, not half as interesting as Dead Horse Canyon from my youth. There were no junk cars, not much garbage. But this diminished stage didn't stop Terry. He strode out in front of the group, carrying more visual props—several oversized posters and maps.

Terry broke us into two arms of observers, and we formed a horseshoe around the head of the gully. Two hundred feet down the steep, wooded slope the gully intersected a deep creek valley running to the west. The landscape here was typical Piedmont woodland, though a little steeper. The hardwoods (oak or hickory) were of a decent age, maybe a hundred years old, so when the Soil Conservation Service folks were here in the 1930s, there was already some tree cover.

One of the scientists, Duke's Dan Richter, a tall, bald, wiry man with a trowel, scrambled down into the gully, raked one wall, and observed the cleared surface up close. "What are you finding, Dan?" Terry asked.

"I'm with you, Terry. I'm happy," Richter added from the depths of the gully and everybody laughed.

I liked Richter right away. I could tell he was one of the leaders of the pack. He had uncovered what was known to soil scientists and geologists as a "soil profile." Soil profiles are not only metaphors, as I tended to use them, but are a long and valuable earth science tradition. They expose a two-dimensional vertical cut through soils, a plane at right angles. Richter had scraped a soil profile onto the gully as readily as I told a story. A soil profile, after scraping, is then inspected for its horizontal arrangement of "horizons," layers parallel to the soil surface whose physical, chemical, and biological characteristics differ from those above or below. In the case of that gully profile, the soil horizons were exposed so Richter, during the gully stop, could deduce more information about the complex situation revealed there. When I first studied geology, I made a metaphoric leap and saw that my own life's periods could be seen as horizons in profile, scraped clean like Richter's soil profiles.

In Richter's soil profile I could see different shifts in the color of the soil. Some were quite easy to distinguish—the thin layer of darker topsoil at the top, the silty red clay in the middle, and the yellow-gray clay at the bottom. Other shifts I knew were more subtle, and, like drinking fine wine, required a palate trained to detect the differences. Soil scientists even taste soil and distinguish between sandy and silty, clay and loam.

There is a connection between soil profiles and my own explorations, but I flip the order of the horizons. When the chronology is reversed, the deepest layers, of which the least can be known, are at the top and more recent layers with more resolution don't appear until the bottom. My first move is always toward verifiable history, but after that, I pause to assess where I can burrow in and imagine. The past is not a place where I pause often on fact-finding missions. I prefer stories with wiggle room. This conjuring of story is how I have trained and elevated my mind, not through verification of fact. The pleasurable work for me is burrowing into, over, under, or around whatever facts I find. This became a habit of mind early on, my default rumination. I have often been rewarded for this storytelling. I have only occasionally been rewarded for getting the answers right on a test, as had so many of those in Terry's research tribe gathered around the first gully.

Terry dished out plenty of facts about the subject at hand. I reminded myself: this was no short story workshop. This is a field lab for a hundred science nerds. The landscape the 1930s scientists had explored opened before us in real time. Terry discussed the dynamics of gullying. Those gathered there in the woods were interested in the real soil science, not so much the metaphoric soil science of my family tree.

For the next few minutes Terry outlined the basics of gullies and their formation—*headward erosion, water flow, nick points, plunge pools, erosional surface, gully caves, base-level.* "I'm just a hand waver, a pointer—I'll try to stick to evidence and not wander off into hypothesis, so you experts jump in at any time," he said in finishing up.

As soon as Terry fell silent the other experts did jump in. For the next twenty minutes the conversation engaged the particulars of that first gully gashed open before us, and everyone tried to wrap their minds around the processes involved in creating it, and in the case of the teachers with students present, wrap the minds of their students around a gully for the first time.

Missy Eppes, a tall professor in a floppy felt hat, looked the part of the field scientist and her expertise showed it: she was fluent with mechanical weathering, soil science, and geomorphology (the study of the form of physical features of the surface of the earth and how they are related to the geology), among other things, and she was an admirable new type of scientist too. Her two children tagged along for the day. They wandered the landscape as we talked and listened to the lecturing, exploring as their mother pried into the intricacies of long-lost field research from the 1930s. I watched as Eppes's children scrambled down into the gully, ran up the side, raced to the very bottom, and waded along a small stream. They were both carrying rock hammers and the whole landscape was a nail. They pounded away at anything resistant.

Deep Family History

"Most of what I will tell you starts with what Mama told me," Sandy began as we rolled toward the hilly ancestral home ground of our Bradley ancestors in Henrietta, North Carolina, an hour north of Spartanburg. Sandy had brought me into her own fieldwork, and I was a willing audience. The conversation was alluvial—our family's story, our lives, Mama's life—laid down by dark waters, depositing the first sediment layers. She was driving and I was taking notes, scrawling, hoping I could read them later, looking for a throughline in our story, one as complex as any story the soil scientists told of the Piedmont. Sandy recounted data about Mama's family, spreading outward and downward, flowing, a freshet of generations.

The Piedmont landscape we drove through was the ground of our being. We counted among our maternal forebears many sharecroppers and tenant farmers who worked this gullied land to exhaustion, and as we drove north, we passed by a few surviving abandoned shacks like those they might have once lived in. The highway followed a ridgeline dividing two river drainages, and gullies fell off on each side. The loss of topsoil was one of the main reasons farmers like our Bradley ancestors abandoned their land, pulled up stakes, and headed into South Carolina to work in cotton mills in the 1920s and 1930s. In the scattered wood lots we passed frequent creamy blooms of genetics gone haywire, escaped and hybridized Bradford pears, flared brightly against the dark spindly hardwoods. In childhood, when this horticultural fiasco of the mass planting of Bradford pears first unfolded, I thought those landscaping trees beautiful that lined the avenues around Spartanburg. Now each renegade blossom became a torch marking our journey into family history.

Sandy is a retired nurse, wife, mother, grandmother, great-grandmother, married for over fifty years. She's eight years my

Columbus Christopher Bradley and Mary Caldonia Beheler,
Spartanburg, S.C. (Photographer Unknown, ca. 1915)

senior, though for the purposes of this inquiry into our shared lives, she functions as both guide and foil against my limited memory of the past. Sandy sits at her computer most days and searches for new facts about our various ancestors. She is a semi-pro genealogist and has been at the search for decades. I say, "facts about our *various* ancestors," because I haven't explained that Sandy is actually my half-sister, and the lines she explores go in multiple directions. We have different fathers, so her father's family story is also one of the founding oral myths of my childhood, since it includes our mutual mother and both our departed fathers. We agreed it was time to write down the stories both of us could still remember.

Our differences are visible. Sandy really *is* sandy compared to me. She has a light complexion and an even-tempered personality. She's like sandy soil, which drains well, and the water is never stagnant. I am more like the heavy red clay of the Piedmont where water stands and the soil becomes saturated. I'm not depressive, but I do hold on to things sometimes longer than I should.

"The Bradleys were the first branch of our family tree that drew my attention when I got interested in family history in the 1980s," Sandy explained. "Back then there was still a multitude of aunts, uncles, and cousins to talk to."

Right away Sandy began to see how complex our story could be. She hit dead ends. She found contradictions. The only thing she could do was continue to research, to push the records back as far as possible, and to gather what family facts she could. She said she often found herself in quagmires of both data and anecdote.

"If I look closely, like a researcher, right away the signals got crossed," she said, "and it's not easy to figure out who we actually were."

Or maybe, by extension, I added, who we are now.

As we drove, Sandy pieced together a brief synopsis of the Bradley line and location. As Sandy told it, our maternal side had for all these generations been full of industry, thrift, vision, luck, callousness, and cunning. She sketched Mama's Bradley family line as a story that played out mainly within the drainage of the Broad River. As we talked, Sandy drove toward the Broad's headwater streams and headed particularly toward High Shoals. Downstream from us, in South Carolina, the great river is simply called the Broad, but just above the North Carolina line the river has two tributary branches, known as the First and Second Broads. The First Broad rises on South Mountain in northeastern Rutherford County and flows southeast into Cleveland County, and then turns southward. There the river passes the city of Shelby, then joins the river just north of the South Carolina line. The Second Broad's origin is further west, near Marion, North Carolina, and it flows southeast into Rutherford County just to the East of Forest City near where it joins the main branch of the Broad. In Colonial times the Broad River in its headwaters was known as the English Broad to distinguish this river from the French Broad that flows west not far away, on the other side of the continental divide, over lands controlled in the eighteenth century by the French.

Sandy said many other family researchers had deduced that two generations of Bradleys had apparently worked at the High Shoals Ironworks on the Second Broad River, pinched hard against the Blue Ridge mountains. The next generations of Bradleys began farming as the ironworks declined. The next two generations were definitely farmers, with the last farming generation moving several dozen miles south of High Shoals to work as tenant farmers in upper Spartanburg County. From there, the children left the farm wholesale, and many went into textile work in Spartanburg. To me all this had sounded like a Piedmont archetype, a Depression-era photograph: Scots-Irish, scrappy, profane, evolving finally into proud cotton mill workers and then into the middle layer of the service economy, ending with people like me, a college professor, and my sister, a nurse. Sandy continued: "I use words like 'deduce,' 'apparently,' and 'likely' because the early census records give hints of the situations of those early Bradleys, but the story the census tells is murky at best."

For years Sandy pored over the census reports. Based on "family research, numerous DNA matches, collaborating stories, written documentation, a growing number of distant cousins have arrived at similar conclusions." Sandy finally settled on the accuracy of the historical written account that a pair of Rutherford County "hammermen" of High Shoals were our ancestors. These men were Thomas Bradley, and his brother, Henry Bradley, whose father was an elder Thomas Bradley. "There are even some that suspect that a Winnie Bradley listed in 1820 as a Free Colored Person, was either the spouse of Thomas, Sr. or possibly a sister. The household listed a male slave aged forty-five or older," Sandy told me. "Could this be Thomas, Sr.? There were three persons listed working in agriculture and two in manufacturing. Could this be the hammermen Thomas and Henry?" As one Bradley cousin told Sandy, the Bradleys "seemed to emerge around 1820 out of nowhere."

Sandy explained what she knew from there: the 1820 census of the area did show Winnie Bradley in High Shoals in a household with seven household members. Two members of the household listed manufacturing as their occupation, but there was no certainty as to what her relation to us might be. Was Willie Bradley an aunt, wife, sister? "It's a genealogical pretzel," Sandy said, laughing.

The iron industry began in New England in the 1640s, then made its way to North Carolina by the 1770s. The site there at High Shoals was established in 1790, founded by Mark Bird, a friend of Benjamin Franklin, and Peter Fisher. Achilles Durham owned the iron factory at High Shoals as it declined from the 1840s onward. Before the introduction of steam power in the 1850s, falling water was the only successful method for operating the bellows and hammers. Dams and sluiceways controlled the flow and directed it over large waterwheels that created the power—hence the positioning on a shoals.

The younger Thomas Bradley was born about 1807 in Rutherford County, North Carolina. He showed up in the census going forward. The earliest of our folks Sandy can solidly locate is the older Thomas. In the census of 1850 when Thomas was listed as a hammerman, he worked across the river at High Shoals. Being a hammerman, Thomas would have worked a heated lump of iron, called a bloom, with a large hammer to drive out the molten slag and produce bar iron. When Sandy first told me that our family was directly connected to the furnaces, I took deep pride in our past. I imagined the raw materials—iron ore, local charcoal, falling water, and heat. I imagined the trip hammer's incessant pounding like an inland tide.

In the case of our family, the census was not the only document we could use to piece together a story. In the 1870s, Christenberry Lee, a circuit preacher from Rutherfordton, reminisced in a newspaper about the old High Shoals ironworks. Lee remembered the ironworks where our ancestors worked as having "three fireplaces at full blast"; laboring there were "three hammermen, one coal-bearer and one to attend to the ore beater, which consisted of a small iron pestle making about three beats per minute." Lee mentioned a Thomas Bradley, Sr., and how, after he retired, his job was passed on to his sons, Thomas, Jr. and Henry. Lee went on to deconstruct the race and lineage of our ancestors. He said the Bradleys, whose names lined up with ours, claimed to be "full-blooded Indians," but as Lee also put it, "the nationality of the Bradly (sic) family was not fully defined. It was well understood that they did not belong to the Anglo-Saxon race."

Then, with a dark but lyrical high note Lee had not hit in any of his earlier reminiscences, he recounted a memory about the first Bradley of whom he had any recollections: "Aunt Winney . . . had in her features some very striking marks of the Indian race. She lived to be very old." Then Lee described our possible ancestor as climbing up the side of her cabin's chimney, placing her feet on projecting rocks, and for unknown reasons, "fastening a hank of thread around the pole, to which the pot hung, and 'swinging off,' committing suicide." The old cabin, in the story Lee recounts, "stood on the hill just a little piece from the big spring between Henrietta No. 1 and No. 2 . . . I do remember how we children used to dread passing this place on our way to school."

In Lee's account there is a hint of our origins and the family hardships to come. I was horrified the first time I read it. I could feel the desperation or despair of the woman hanging herself and knew I would never get to the bottom of this psychosis of which no genealogist or historian could ever sketch an outline. I remember worrying that a tendency toward melancholy and suicide might come at me not only from my father's side, but my mother's as well. How much might the past determine the present? The legacy of mixed heritage can be psychological as well as physical.

"The real problem," Sandy went on, "is who were the Bradleys actually and where were they?" Then she explained how the census works to determine an area's population, something I had only limited experience with. "The census simply counts people through the years. Tracing the complexity of our family takes patience." This patience was something Sandy had developed through decades working with the census forms.

After an hour we left Highway 221 and turned onto the Henrietta Road, and cruised down toward the Second Broad River. When we approached Henrietta, Sandy stopped the car on the west side of the river so I could take in the scene at the old dam. I was hoping for a kindly Bradley visitation from the past, but my imagination stalled quickly at the chain link bordering the Baptist church parking lot next to the Second Broad River bridge.

Sandy waited by the car in a drizzle. The river, high and loud from recent rains, washed out Sandy's census explanation of the past and focused me on the present. Beyond the rusted fence was a blind of dormant winter vines and stunted riverside saplings rooted only in a scree of loose riprap. At the foot of the fill-slope the old stone dam and the gneiss shoals were stained black and clay-colored. I tried my best to conjure the past, but the river's real roar was the only available dissonant music.

"What did you see?" Sandy asked when I returned to the car.

"The river descending in curdled spume from the silted mill pond to the splattering rocks below," I said. "And the rushing gray-green flow that had long ago powered the bellows."

We drove on across the bridge into Henrietta proper, as Sandy began to review the deep swirl of our identity. "Some family sources stated that Thomas's son Leeson married a cousin, Millie, also a Bradley. Millie's parents, Henry (our four times great grandfather, but also a five times great uncle) and Naomi Downey, were also enumerated differently during the censuses. Henry's family were

Free Colored Persons in 1840, mulatto in 1850, not listed in 1860, and white in 1870. In 1880, Leeson and Millie's family was listed as Indian. But in 1900 the census taker recorded them as Black," Sandy explained. "The next time I found Millie was in 1920 and she has become white along with her daughters. Leeson Bradley was living with a Thomas Bradley in 1850 and was enumerated mulatto, as were the remaining household members. This Thomas was assumed to be Leeson's father as family elders had named him. In the 1830 and 1840 censuses the header of the census page stated, 'Free Colored Persons.' Thomas was mulatto again in 1860 but listed as white in 1870."

Several people through the years have asked Sandy whether the Bradleys might be Melungeons, legendary descendants of people of mixed European, African, and Native American ancestry usually found in the area where Tennessee, Virginia, and North Carolina converge.

"An aunt once heard that our two-times-great grandmother Mary Caldonia Beheler Bradley's mother Dulcenda came from an area up there called Indian Head," Sandy said. "I just wrote it all down. I can't prove any of it."

I wasn't looking for proof. I was looking for story and Sandy was giving me plenty. The stories got me thinking more deeply about Mama's family and its connection to this landscape. These deep family connections had activated my storytelling brain only a few hundred yards from where the community of High Shoals had once thrived. I loved the powerful idea that soil was once life for the vast majority of people living on the land, including my people.

When Sandy stopped on the other side of the bridge, I stepped out and looked through a fence at the old mill site, now a junk yard. Under all the accumulated scrap had been the ironworks village where the first hammermen Bradleys had worked and dwelled. Somewhere else between the bridge and the town of Caroleen up-stream, old Aunt Winney Bradley had hung herself off her cabin mantel with a hank of yarn.

Besides the story of Aunt Winney's tragic death, the story of her "Indian features" had always activated some curiosity deep in me. There had always been an oral history of Indian ancestry in our family, something not so unusual among white southerners. My knowledge of story stretches back as far as I can remember. It guides some of my own sense of identity. In high school my nickname was Savage because of my dark skin, and I was even part of a troupe of Boy Scout Indian dancers with our own outfits.

Of course, Sandy was always well aware that judgments of race were made by a lone census taker visiting the house. Sandy always warned me that so much about the Bradleys was speculation. It was I, mostly, who ran with the stories.

Even though Sandy saw how complex these issues could be, as she moved deeper into genealogy, she looked for the Indian and ignored all the rest. She formed her own questions about the Bradleys based on what she found in the census records, but it was very confusing. Why did the census say "M" in one place, and "B" in another? She found out that white, Black, mulatto were the standard terms by 1850–60. Before that the categories were free whites, slaves, free people of color. It wasn't until the 1870 census that she began to see "Indian" regularly, though "I" did occur scattered through earlier census records. All they had was "WBM," or white, Black, mulatto.

She kept going back and back. Then Sandy started corresponding with other Bradleys, descended from the elder Thomas's other son, Henry, and that's when she started to hear the stories about them maybe being Black. When I hear the early story of our family, I begin to see how much is buried there. Here was a story that had stayed hidden deep in our family for a century. Sandy said some of the family wouldn't even talk about it. This complex identity was off-limits.

Sandy wasn't afraid to dig deeper and interrogate the census data. The 1830 census listed the younger Thomas Bradley as "not a slave," but as a "free-colored male." In 1840 he appeared as "a free-colored person," and in 1850, as a "mulatto." Thomas's son Leeson was listed as "mulatto" in 1850 and 1860, and in the 1870 census Leeson's son Columbus Christopher was listed as mulatto, then in 1880, as "Indian," but as white between 1900 and 1920.

What effect had this transition by my great-great-grandfather Columbus Christopher Bradley in 1900 exercised on me? I had no doubt that the poverty that my mother's family has struggled with for a century was lessened by Lum Bradley's whiteness. Had he remained of mixed race in the census he would have been subject to Jim Crow laws and even the threat of lynching. His whiteness protected his family for generations—and by extension, protected and enriched me.

People I knew growing up who considered themselves white often alleged other people had nonwhite ancestry, usually Native American or Black. When that was said, it was always said as if it created a scandal or shamed the other person. I can't recall feeling either scandal or shame. I loved the stories about our mixed ancestry, and I often told them for their own sake. I was never made to suffer on my story's account. I'm curious and follow my story's flow. When I tell of the Bradleys' mixed identity, I feel positive about being a part of the complex story of the South, a place where much mixing has taken place, especially between white Europeans and Black Africans.

My dark skin is the clue to why my story is what it is. My wife Betsy once described me as "olive with a hint of pink." A Black friend went one step further. He said that when he showed a photo of me taken in high school to his wife and daughter, they claimed I could "pass." I joked that passing was a family tradition, going back many generations, highlighting the rich broth Mama's family cooked up as the nineteenth century turned to the twentieth.

In contrast, Sandy could tan, but she had to do it slowly. Mama never burned. Neither did I. In spite of her fair skin, Sandy remembered that she was proud of that hint of Indian blood when she first learned of it. Before I was born, my Daddy, John Lane, took Mama and Sandy on a trip from Southern Pines to the town of Cherokee, North Carolina, where they saw the play "Unto These Hills." Sandy said she was drawn to the Indians because of the stories. She felt connected in some way to them. In a picture of Mama after they returned from Florida in 1948, Sandy was propped up on Mama's hip. Sandy said she looked "dark as an Indian."

There are other stories of the Bradleys and their mysterious identity. A cousin told Sandy he would go up to Cherokee and people would stop him and ask if he was an Indian. He was up there with a female cousin one time and somebody asked her for help in a tourist shop. "I don't work here," she answered. "Oh, I thought you were Indian," the other tourist said. It made her furious.

Another time the cousin was at Bradley Falls near Saluda, North Carolina, and someone there said, "You're one of those Bradley Indians," and he answered, "Well, I am a Bradley, but I haven't been able to prove I'm an Indian."

Sandy said Mama always clung to the belief that it was "Indian blood" that resulted in our dark complexions. But Indians weren't thought of very well back then, and so for Mama it would have been "a taint" to have either Indian or Black ancestry. When Sandy told her what she'd found, Mama listened but did not comment. Mama always said, "I was told" . . . and continued to claim that Indian blood.

Complexion comes from the Latin, *complectere*, to "embrace or comprise." On early twentieth-century military registration forms the complexion choices were "sallow, light, ruddy, dark, freckled, light brown, dark brown, and black." White as a race, geneticists say, is entirely political. It is one of the byproducts of the racist mind. I waded into these waters carefully, trying not to go so deep that I lose sight of where I stepped. I grew up "white," with its privileges and complexities. In my youth, because of food stamps and our crappy houses, I thought of myself as "poor white." I never thought deeply about my genetics until the information Sandy discovered.

DNA tests, and the data they provided, added to our story. Both Sandy and I have swabbed our cheeks, placed our saliva in a tube, and mailed the samples off to DNA labs. Being half-siblings, we shared 24.2 percent of our DNA. With the results each of us formed a story. I am 95.9 percent northern European. Of that, 49.4 percent is British and Irish, 30.1 percent French and German, and 2.4 percent Italian. What I tended to focus on was the 1.1 percent West African that showed up. Sandy was primarily Northern European as well, but had a healthy infusion of 8.6 percent Scandinavian, maybe the Viking inheritance of her blond father. Interestingly, her West African was only 0.5 percent and there was 0.2 percent Native American. Black cousins show up in both of our 23andMe inboxes. So far there haven't been any Native Americans.

"It's like dealing cards," Sandy explained. "Your mother gives you a card and your father gives you another. You could have received a double dose from your mother and your father, two cards, not one."

Who am I? What are we? Who was I as a child and who am I now? It shouldn't be lonely looking back through time, but it sure could be. Often you find the ridgetops barren of facts, yet stories hide in the underbrush. The census records left me wanting. It was only when I approached the present that the factual resolution becomes clear enough to claim anything for sure. Accounting for family stories was not like surveying level land. My sister and I could settle on some observations but differ on others. We recited the chronicle that each of us remembered, the buried valleys and gullies that still creased our daily lives. We both had images we followed in order to journey back from the edge. I curated a heap of family stories. Sandy curated hers too, and she also had the photos, the census records, the deeds, and the maps to pin it all down. My sister's mind was like a high-resolution map of kinship. I looked forward to braiding our memories, to uncovering more of what we both knew and remembered.

I stared into the old mill site, a fenced mess of abandoned rags, rubble brick, and ruined walls. Wrecked trucks seemed to be the only active industry. A barking German shepherd on a five-foot chain warned me to keep my distance. Her attentive free-range puppy seemed more curious than threatened. I turned around. Try as I might, I couldn't close the cluttered gap between our family story and such a stunted present sleeping soundly under fifty years of Henrietta's grimy squalor. That was as close as I could get to the storied High Shoals Ironworks.

The rest of our trip we spent communing with the dead, paying tribute to the ancestors by visitation. Four generations of our people are settled among the nearby Goodes Creek Baptist and Kistler's Chapel cemeteries. We entered each cemetery and scouted the rows of stones until we could locate those associated with the Bradleys. The area around Henrietta is ruined now, but it endures as home. Even after they died near Spartanburg my great-great-grandparents and great-grandparents were brought back up there to be buried. Sandy said that when she started coming up in the 1980s the oldest Bradleys were still dressing the graves. Such commitment to place and the dead is rare today. I feel I have it. I have practiced a sort of ancestor worship my whole life. Standing by Columbus Christopher Bradley's headstone I felt both a completion and a springboard to the future. I felt great hope when I saw how solid his stone was, how deeply chiseled his name and dates, the epitaph—"He sleepeth"—, and how well tended was his plot still. The Bradleys had done all right.

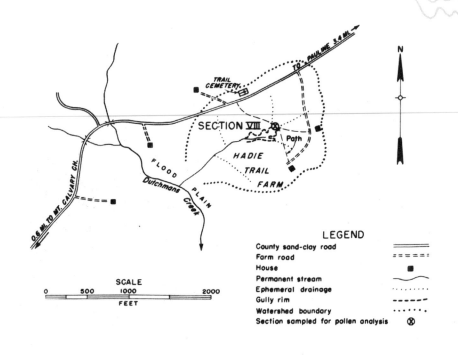

Map of Trail Gully Property (Created by Soil Conservation Service, 1930s)

Marshall Tucker Gully

"We are now as ever in times of continual change," Terry likes to say, being an heir of John Harrington. After leaving the Big Lots shopping center we changed locations, convoying ten miles down Highway 56 to visit gully number two, the second stop of Terry's Friends of the Pleistocene field trip. This place was officially called The Trail Gully, named for Hattie Trail, who owned the property. Hoye Eargle and others did research there in the late 1930s. Terry walked us into the woods again, and we looked into the gully. In the bottom lay a jumbled and broken structure—beams, boards, and tin. The gully had been owned in the 1970s and 1980s by Toy and Tommy Caldwell of Marshall Tucker Band fame. Terry stood at the gully's apex and explained the logic of the Tucker Boys: "They tore an old house down. 'What do we do with it? I know. Throw it in the gully!' So they pushed an old wooden farmhouse in, obscuring one of the best sites to observe the buried organic deposits."

Besides the presence of the buried organic deposits in the landscape at the bottom of buried valleys, the most intriguing question for Hoye Eargle and other scientists working in the 1930s on "the Piedmont problem" was how did these buried deposits get buried, as material burying them was not "alluvium," or material transported, deposited by flowing water. The soils covering these buried organic deposits were layers of "colluvium," suggesting the valleys and closed depressions were filled in by soils moving downslope chiefly by soil creep, slumping, frost action, and sheet wash over time. Eargle described the nature of the colluvial deposits as "generally massive, poorly sorted, and firm, sandy clay or clayey sand."

All of this information felt a little like colluvial layers to me. I had always believed the origin myth of the Piedmont, that the region was one of the world's great stable land surfaces, that it was shaped over millions of years mostly by the work of stream dissection and deep weathering. Erosion in this model had been slow, working on soils that have mostly been formed in place—"residual" as they are called. Having that as the myth of my place had given me stability too. I come from a place slow to change.

Eargle had published a gully soil profile, and Terry reproduced it in his field guide. "Turn to page fourteen," he yelled and explained that twenty feet below the surface was the buried organic deposit, described by the soil men in one of their reports as "more bluish, except when close to incorporated logs and other organic matter. Logs up to 12 inches (30 cm) in diameter in the lower half appear to be oak and conifer. Acorns and hickory nuts were found . . . organic layer . . . sharp and undulating."

Terry waved his arms about, narrating the work done here by the soil men, but I could sense it was finally dawning on folks how radical that gully work was back in the 1930s and how many questions the buried valleys and their "buried organic deposits" could raise.

"Can pollen migrate?" someone yelled.

"Generally not; pollen is usually trapped in the layers where it is formed," Terry said.

Richter yelled, "Loosen up our minds, Terry."

My mind was loose, but I was still having trouble keeping up with the intellectual ping pong match. It had been almost forty years since my three college geology classes, and I'd only traveled as an educated tourist in the world of earth science ever since. This discussion wasn't sitting on a tailgate with Terry explaining the landscape to a poet. These were professionals, intent on reviewing the evidence laid out before them.

The question about pollen had to do with what is trapped in the organic deposits. I'd read that one way to recover a landscape's deep past is to identify the pollen from vegetation and to map its dispersal. Tree pollen can spread widely since the blooms can be so far above the ground; shrubs and flowers not so far, but their pollen does travel, hence its presence in the buried organic deposits in the gullies. The paleo-pollen survives buried, often in stratified layers of sediment, but it is tiny, often only a few cells.

Terry had also told me pollen could be used to date the deposits, something that could provide information about a changing climate through time.

Geologists like Eargle knew about deep time, but radiocarbon dating wasn't developed until the 1940s, so he was unable to precisely date anything he found. He would have had to look at changes in vegetation. The evidence presented by Terry through the pollen had been found by Eargle in the buried organic deposits. "The idea is that if you have northern species of plants growing here, you had a different climate, so the deposits must have been from the Pleistocene or earlier," Terry explained.

I heard the word *climate* and I was transported back to a colder place, like northern Minnesota. When these deposits were likely laid down it was a glacial time, when an ice wall a mile high had advanced into what is now central Pennsylvania, deeply cooling my now temperate Piedmont.

"This is a filled valley, and the colluvium is more resistant than alluvium."

I knew alluvium to be sediment that has been deposited on beaches, on lake shores, and by streams.

"Three feet down is the boundary of the Holocene and Pleistocene. The interval between three and a half feet and ten feet below the surface was laid down between sixty and seventy thousand years. There's twenty-five feet of colluvium sitting on top of saprolite and there are organic sediments over one hundred thousand years old."

We formed a loose interrogating horseshoe around the gully classroom like one of those stadium lecture halls for anatomy you see in medical schools. In our case the gully was the cadaver, and Terry was the professor gesturing at the subject. Richter stood on one side and Eppes on the other; she listened and played polite devil's advocate to Terry's lecturing professor. "Could the fill be some paleo-river sand and gravel?" Eppes asked. "What is the evidence that this is colluvium?"

"Maybe we should call this group Friends of the Pliocene," Richter inserted, making a geologic time scale joke, suggesting the deposits might be millions of years older than the Pleistocene.

Terry said the soil men had "found little evidence of cross-bedding in the colluvium that would suggest alluvial deposits." The published report, he explained, noted the deposits are "massive, poorly sorted, and firm," Terry concluded and pointed to the deposits in the gully.

Eppes heard Terry out and then turned and whispered an impromptu interpretive lecture for her students, all gathered close. She plunged into the detail and complexity of soils and Piedmont geology and how difficult it really was to sort out what was going on in these sites. She warned against jumping to any conclusions, trying to make it easier for her undergrads to understand what was happening in the gully and why everyone was so argumentative about gullies.

Some folks descended into the gully on an aluminum ladder to look up close at the soil profile, while others took the more exciting route and slid down the gully walls to the floor and advanced on the exposed soil like pilgrims. "Be careful," Terry yelled. "That old house was built with nails, you know."

I meandered around the gully rim and paused where one young soil scientist looked perplexed by the evidence before him. I asked him if buried organic deposits pointed him toward evidence for an exciting new conception of how the Piedmont land surface had been formed.

"I did my doctorate on the formation of Piedmont and was taught that this landscape was the most stable land surface on earth," he said, "and now that paradigm has shifted in one day."

Another friend of the Pleistocene wandered over, and the first scientist told him what he was thinking. Scientist number two smiled wryly and said, "These filled valleys are interesting, but they may be a merely local phenomenon of the upper Piedmont and therefore can be explained by their steeper Pleistocene valley slopes and proximity to mountain front." He wasn't ready to shift anybody's paradigm. "What would shift your thinking?" I asked.

"More data."

Data be damned. When Terry first handed me an account of the buried organic deposits a few weeks before the field trip, I had been awash with the imaginative possibilities, and now in the field, I ran with them. The account of the 1940 field trip described how those present argued about the origin of these very deposits and one of the explanations was known as "the beaver-pond theory." The buried organic deposits were generally in valley heads where waters were quiet and not subject to flooding, which may have suggested a selection of site by the animals; it seemed that the wooded material came to rest by "slow accretion." The trunks of the trees the scientists observed were mostly lying across where the stream would have flowed, and there were big blocks of peat and clay, as if a dam might have broken and the mass carried downstream.

What felled the logs? Maybe the agent of the felling could have been one of my favorite extinct mammals, the giant beavers of the Pleistocene. *Castoroides* were the largest rodents ever to exist. They ranged all over North America and could grow to seven and a half feet long and weigh two hundred and fifty pounds. Was it possible to recover some of these logs and look for the gnaw marks? The smooth slices of their six-inch incisors?

Or maybe the buried organic deposits were linked to *Castoroides*'s smaller cousin, *Castor Canadensis*, a common mammal that persisted through the Holocene into our era, and now, through reintroduction, was once again at work transforming the small creek valleys of the Piedmont. Whether or not there were beaver dams, or beaver gnaw marks in the buried organic deposits, it was easy to project a mental image of a landscape puddled with active beaver ponds in steep-sided Pleistocene valleys hypothesized by those early researchers.

While his number one van driver (I) was lost nearby in Pleistocene beaver reveries, Terry answered a few more straightforward queries from nearby spectators, realizing that whatever else happened at gully number two, it would unfold informally in teams of twos, threes, or more. Terry shifted from lecturer to policeman, and his forty years of teaching field geology and crowd management at sites that could be hazardous kicked in. "Could you all on the left side of the gully please move back from that undercut edge?" he yelled with more seriousness than ever before. "I don't want any major slumping events here."

Our Great-grandmother Ella Mabe Bradley, Fairmont, S.C.
(Photographer Unknown, 1936)

Chinquapins

Our mother's grandmother Ella Mabe was from Carroll County, Virginia, a mountainous region hard up against the North Carolina line. Ella was born on a hill farm there in 1886. Ella was one of four children that John David Mabe fathered with his first wife. John David then married two other women and fathered eight half-siblings to Ella. When I head down these genealogical backroads with Sandy it always helps to have a chart before me. It would be years before I finally compiled the four lines of my mother's family into a working mind map of kinship. Sandy seemed to remember it all. "I don't remember everything, Johnny," Sandy would counter. "I have to pull up my records. That's what I rely on to keep myself straight."

In 1903 Ella Mabe was seventeen when she met a local widowed farmer named James B. Williams who had at least four children. Williams was thirty years Ella's senior. "People married out of necessity back then," Sandy explained. "He likely needed somebody to take care of all those kids." Ella and John Williams had a stillborn infant in 1905, but soon after, the marriage dissolved. Then Ella left Carroll County. Sandy heard that Ella left with another local couple and that they were all going to California. In the first decade of the twentieth century going out there was known as "The California Dream."

"The next we know for sure Ella was not in California, but instead she was working in Spartanburg where she married our great-grandfather John Simeon Bradley in the Spartan Mills village in 1908. I thought it was fascinating that Ella took off, and went so far away," Sandy explained.

A few weeks earlier on the way back from Virginia I stopped in Hillsville. It was a place where the vistas could not be confused for my native Piedmont. It was Appalachia instead of Piedmont. In all four directions every long view was closed in by high and sharp ridges, wooded after they rise, too steep to farm.

I have a picture of Ella, but at that time, I had never met another Mabe. The Mabe stories came down to me through Sandy, yet Mabe genes comprise one-eighth of my genetic map. There is some psychic good to be found in recreating the 110-year-old story of a great-grandmother's migration from the farming world of Virginia to an early industrial textile village of the Carolina Piedmont. I would learn something by chasing this family spirit to ground.

After I had pulled off I-77 I visited the family cemetery. "You can't miss it," Sandy had told me. She was right. The cemetery was neatly tended with about fifty graves. Sandy said Mabe reunions were always held in the front yard of an old house across the street where a cousin named Ira Mabe once lived. Ira Mabe died in 1940 but the house still stands, a gray, once elegant two-story with crumbling front balconies on each floor. It was now used for storage; the boxwoods were untrimmed and a catawba tree sprawled in the side yard. A rust-red early 1950s-era International Harvester farm pickup with flat tires and a spare on the running board rested under a walnut tree.

In the cemetery there were many Mabes. There were small "grandma" and "grandpa" signs, various ceramic cherubs, and tended artificial flowers. I almost expected to see the old late spring or summer mountain tradition, where each grave is topped with a mound of white sand or gravel, and family members stick flowers in the mound on "Decoration Day" as the tradition was called.

After I had left the cemetery, I drove back toward I-77 and turned back on Oak Grove as Sandy had instructed me. She said I could view the old farm from the parking lot of the Woodlawn Church of God. Next door was where an elderly cousin and his wife had lived. Sandy said she and Mama had stayed with them for a Mabe family reunion in 1989.

I sensed right away I was in a high spot, a perfect place for an old house. The land receded steeply to the West in pasture, broken here and there by lines of hardwoods and creased deeply by three spring runs. Next to the church I noticed a man completing chores at a house tucked behind the trees, loading bags of garbage likely for a run to the dump. I introduced myself and explained the family pilgrimage I was on. He said his wife was a Mabe, and yes, she was the granddaughter of Harry Mabe. That was his house in the trees. They'd added onto it since they'd moved in.

Once our cousin's husband determined I was kin, at least by marriage, he opened up a little. "We own thirty-three acres of the old farm and still make hay on the steep pastures, though I played years in a band and now work robotics third shift at the Volvo truck plant up the interstate in Pulaski."

How about "the old Mabe home place"? He pointed to where the pasture fell off. There had been a Mabe house that burned just in front of us "where that cherry tree is."

"That's where Harry Mabe grew up, but that's not 'the home place.' The home place is in the trees to our East on land owned now by another cousin. We got four-wheeler trails up through there and I don't know if the foundation's still visible but there are boxwoods."

Not a dozen miles south of the farm, Coulston Church Road intersects Highway 221, or the Carrollton Pike, one of the old central market routes southwest out of the mountains into the Piedmont. Parts of Highway 221 through the mountains in southwest Virginia are now marketed as the Crooked Road, a route to discover old-time music. That crooked route was maybe what our great-grandmother took out of Carroll County down into the Piedmont. It was a long way, over a hundred miles, before curvy 221 actually descended from the high country and finally switched back dramatically down the escarpment above Marion, North Carolina, following the Linville River and then entering South Carolina.

Ella likely left the farm on foot, in a wagon, or on a mule. Cars weren't common in 1906. There were only a few other routes Ella and her traveling companions could have taken. North would have taken them to Floyd and deeper into the mountains. The more direct route was east of Hillsville, then down into the Virginia Piedmont, Highway 58, back then likely still called the Danville Pike; or they could have gone west and continued through the Cumberland Gap like pioneers of old.

Another possible route out of Carroll County would have been up to the nearest rail line, fifteen miles north, the Virginia and Tennessee, a line that would have gone to Bristol; and from there Ella could have found her way to Asheville and then on down to Spartanburg. It is so much easier to move around today. Hillsville is only three hours by interstate from Spartanburg. The interstate is so painless usually—just turn on a podcast and go. When Ella left the farm the trip would have taken days.

Whatever way Ella came out of the mountains, she definitely met our great-grandfather John Simeon Bradley after she arrived in Spartanburg. He was ten years older and was himself a farm refugee, but from Rutherford County. He had been married before and, like Ella's own father, had four children by the early marriage. John Simeon Bradley and Ella Mabe married in January of 1908, and for the next thirty years John Bradley worked in various Piedmont mills.

The ties between Hillsville and Spartanburg must have remained strong through Ella.

Mama never lost touch with the Mabe side of the family. She visited the old Mabe farm with her mother, sister, stepfather Jim Norris, and the Norris half-brothers and sisters for more reunions when she was a child during the late 1930s. She told Sandy she remembered having to ford a small stream on the driveway into the property.

The spring where Ella once dipped water still rises at the head of Staunton Branch, which crosses the road just west of the cemetery and Ira Mabe's old house. My cousin's husband had said he'd thought about building a dam and creating a small pond there. As we talked, we stood in the old roadbed that passed close by the Mabes' house. "The new road is about twenty yards in front of this old one. The house had originally been a cow barn and in the basement was once a concrete trough for feeding cows," he said.

Sandy said she visited Harry Mabe and his wife decades ago. She descended into the basement to see Bertha's canned goods stored there amid the trough and canning tables.

"We tore that trough out when we renovated the house," our cousin's husband said.

He scanned the brush along the edge of the driveway, reached out and picked something. "Chinquapins," he said and showed me the green flurry of burrs at the ends of the dark green, alternate-leafed branches of the shrub. He located two or three of the little brown acorns and showed how to crack them open with his teeth and eat them. "They're like a chestnut. The squirrels will get them the moment the burrs open. They're rare now but we got them all up through here. When Harry was in the hospital before he died, I used to take him handfuls of Chinquapins."

Montgomery Building, Downtown Spartanburg, S.C.
(Photographer Unknown, 1930s; Spartanburg Herald-Journal
Collection, Spartanburg County Public Libraries)

Restoration

The ten-story Montgomery Building rose in downtown Spartanburg on the former site of textile baron Captain John Montgomery's Church Street residence, a two-story Victorian with wisteria vines shading the south-facing porch. Montgomery died in 1902, and his three sons received the property from his estate. In 1924 they transferred the large lot to Montgomery Building, Inc. At the groundbreaking for Spartanburg's first "skyscraper" that same year, a steam shovel dug a large hole and pushed the family home into it, much as the Marshall Tucker band members would dispose of another old house fifty years later. The city fathers thought they were merely filling up a low place with the remnants of the past. Over this "buried organic deposit" in the heart of downtown rose a spectacular building that played a huge part in the soil story of Spartanburg.

The Montgomery Building was designed by Lockwood Greene & Company, an architectural and engineering firm from Boston. The skeletal steel building was built in the Chicago style. The building's façade was faced with limestone, featuring Renaissance Revival detailing. In both main entrances tall bays with base-relief molding featured urns filled with fruit. On the parapet above these bays a crest featured the letter "M."

The building was the tallest structure in Spartanburg until the 1950s. Mama walked past it many times. Back then Spartanburg was a city of almost forty thousand, with hotels, theaters, and department stores lining the streets. Nights when the soil men drove in from the countryside, they could see the Montgomery Building glowing like a lighthouse above downtown's brick stores and offices.

During its heyday from the twenties to 1960s, tenants found the building most desirable. Many textile companies rented downtown offices there, as would be expected with the Montgomery family's influence. Pacolet Manufacturing Company, Inman Mills, the South Carolina Cotton Manufacturing Association, Arcadia Mills, the Carolina Cotton Association, the American Spinning company, and Deering-Milliken all had offices in the building at one time. Years later, with the building almost empty, my wife Betsy accepted free office space for her literary arts organization, and when I went up to see her, I often ran into a man named Harry Gibson in the elevator going down. Mr. Gibson was a ninety-year-old, stogie-smoking coal broker who had kept an office in the building since it opened. I lacked the foresight to ask Mr. Gibson about the history of the building and the Soil Conservation Service in particular. That was years before my interest in gullies.

In August of 1933, eight years after the Montgomery Building opened, the Southern Regional Office of the Soil Erosion Service (SES) took up residence. In 1935 the SES became the Soil Conservation Service (SCS). Later, at its apex in the early 1940s, the Southern Regional Office of the SCS employed two hundred full-time workers and occupied a full floor. The SCS had a large motor pool and brought a steady pulse of highly educated professionals to Spartanburg, including those conducting the gully research.

The first head of both the SES and the SCS up in Washington was Hugh Hammond Bennett, a chemist and soil scientist. Bennett had been born and raised in North Carolina. As a firsthand witness to soil erosion he became an evangelist against soil erosion. He had spent the 1920s promoting and fighting a war against the destruction. He was a master of rhetoric, and used his growing bully pulpit to the advantage of the cause. His 1928 USDA bulletin coauthored with William Ridgely Chapline, entitled *Soil Erosion: A National Menace*, finally aroused national attention where others had failed. Once he had attention and funding, Bennett encouraged applied research on methods like terracing of gullied fields for immediate benefit to farmers. As head of the Soil Conservation Service, Bennett selected sites, designed research programs, and established best practices—for crops, climates, soils, and geographies.

This first generation of soil experts to arrive in Spartanburg County had grand expectations and evangelical zeal. As part of the original national push the Soil Erosion Service established the South's first erosion control demo project, the South Tyger River Erosion Control Project, in Spartanburg County. In fall of 1933 Dr. T. S. Buie was named as its administrator. In an article about the project, Buie echoed the rhetoric of his superior, Hugh Hammond Bennett, describing erosion: "An enemy as real as any our troops ever have faced in battle has conquered an area 35,000,000 acres in extent, laid waste to what once were fertile fields and almost unchallenged continues his relentless march of destruction across other fields wherever the slope of the land is sufficient for water to flow."

The South Tyger River Project was mammoth—one hundred and ten thousand acres in two counties (Spartanburg and Greenville), employing twenty experts on farm engineering, soils, crops, and forestry and three hundred laborers. Six hundred and eight farms were improved by new techniques like terracing in Spartanburg County alone. The purpose of the project was twofold, according to Dr. Buie—to check existing erosion ("control gullies already formed and the prevention of their further spread") and to teach farmers to adopt tilling methods that would help prevent future soil loss. "Our program calls for extensive reforestation of the steeper slopes" and the planting of all other acreage in "more or less permanent crops," Dr. Buie wrote. Terraces and strip-cropping also would be employed, the first major use of those methods in the Southeast.

Major gully control was the first effort of the program. The men used as laborers for this gully work were drawn from the relief rolls of the counties. This was a year or so before the establishment of the Civilian Conservation Corps camps in Spartanburg County and the formal partnership for the utilization of labor from those camps.

The Soil Conservation Service was divided into two subunits, the Office of Operations and the Office of Research. The Office of Operations consisted of the practical work of demonstration projects, drainage and irrigation work, building check dams to stop field erosion, tending nurseries for plants, directing extension agencies, and other day-to-day activities of the Service. But Aldo Leopold, Carl O. Sauer, and others argued for the importance of research to fully understand landscape problems. Accordingly, the Office of Research created five research divisions relating to these problems. Two of these divisions, the Climatic and Physiographic Division and the Sedimentation Division, worked intensely in Spartanburg County from 1936 until 1941 to improve the knowledge of the ruined landscapes of the upper Piedmont. Based on the recommendations of Sauer, the Climatic and Physiographic Division focused their work on understanding the environmental and geologic factors involved in gully formation and filled valleys. The Sedimentation Division focused its research efforts on understanding sediment dynamics and accumulation in Piedmont stream valleys.

The Soil Conservation Service also hired talented locals. One employee in the late 1930s was Mary Ellen Suitt, a young woman just graduated from Ringling School of Art, who had returned home to Spartanburg. She was a gifted visual artist, but she had no drafting skills because Spartanburg High School didn't allow girls to take mechanical drawing. When she was hired, she was given an ink jar, a pen, and sent home to draw a sample plat of a farm. Suitt ended up working thirty-three years for the Soil Conservation Service, including top secret work in the Montgomery Building on military maps during World War II. She always prided herself in being only one of several women cartographers in a world dominated by men.

Suitt never married but traveled widely, and became a well-known local artist. She painted watercolors of Piedmont landscapes, and near the end of her life, in her nineties, she was known for her paintings of people with blue skin. The Mary Ellen Suitt story reminds me of Terry's mother's—young Southern women with lots of art talent and an interest in local landscapes. Had Terry's mother not met and married his father, her life might have mirrored the life of Mary Ellen Suitt.

By the time my wife Betsy moved into a Montgomery Building office in 2000 the former showplace was on the verge of condemnation. There was no sign at all of the Soil Conservation Service. Later, developers from Charleston bought the building and completely renovated it. Crews worked to remove thousands of sections of limestone cladding and installed new cast-concrete pieces to replicate the originals. Craftsmen replaced old windows with four hundred mahogany ones to match the originals removed decades ago. The restored building now has retail, dining, office space, and sixty-three residential apartments. Every time I see the building, I wish that Piedmont gullies were as easily renovated as ninety-year-old skyscrapers.

When I drive past the Montgomery Building, I think about the work done there for decades by the Soil Conservation Service. When I stop at the light out front, I try to read the silver historical plaque across the street, but the signal is never red long enough. One day I turned and parked behind the building and walked to the front. Cutting from the parking lot in the back to Church Street, I passed through a small garden with fragments of the original façade embedded in a flower bed—broken medallions, half a crested tablet.

The historic plaque itself left me disappointed. I wanted a loving tribute to the Soil Conservation Service, the large, important New Deal government agency that worked so long and hard to "save" the fields of the South. Instead, the marker is dedicated to the National Association of Soil Conservation Districts, a private enterprise created in Chicago in 1946 and given its first office in the Montgomery Building that same year. Not that the idea of soil conservation districts isn't important. I just expected more celebration for the whole service. I hoped for some mention of the work done by the Climatic and Physiographic Division of Soil Conservation Service on those mysterious buried organic deposits, but no such luck. The scs obviously lacked advocates that the Districts possessed. There is little permanent celebration of the scs's life and scientific legacy in Spartanburg. In all my searching I couldn't even determine which floor held the offices the soil people had worked in.

I waited in the dusky winter light to cross Church Street, and there I had a strange, enriching vision of the past. Streaming out of the two tall entrance bays were the soil men and women mingling with the cotton and coal brokers, the middle management men from the textile companies, and a hundred others bumping into the secretaries and cartographers, the salesmen and the clerks. They surged and spread out onto the sidewalk like spirits, dressed in worsted suits and print dresses, wearing dark fedoras and bright scarves. They bought evening papers from venders and checked their watches before moving on toward home. They left behind the day's figures and data, the office business and the intellectual chores meant to run a town and an agency. Decades later Terry would bring them back to me through reports and maps and introduce me to their minds.

B. Horizon

*Commonly referred to as subsoil,
a deeper zone of accumulation where
rainwater percolates through and
leaches material from above.
The material is weathered in place.*

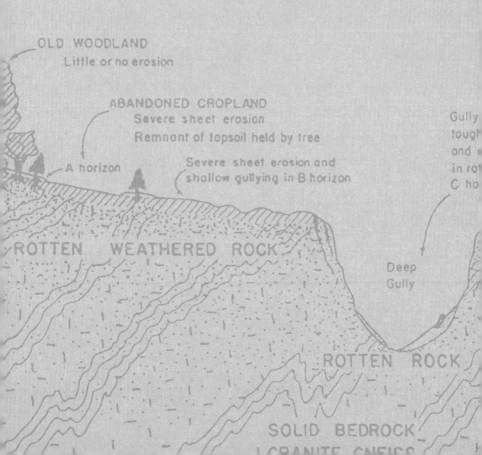

OLD WOODLAND
Little or no erosion

ABANDONED CROPLAND
Severe sheet erosion
Remnant of topsoil held by tree

A horizon

Severe sheet erosion and
shallow gullying in B horizon

Gully
tough
and
in ro
C ho

ROTTEN   WEATHERED   ROCK

Deep
Gully

ROTTEN   ROCK

SOLID   BEDROCK

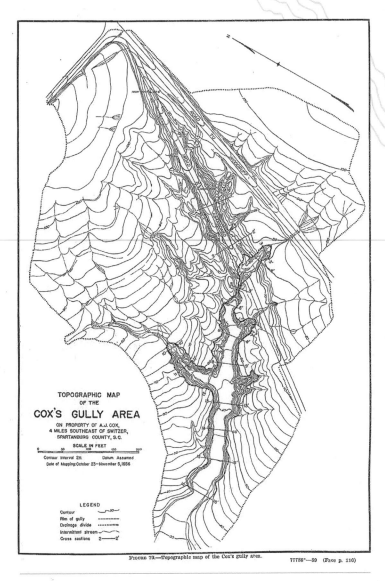

TOPOGRAPHIC MAP
OF THE
COX'S GULLY AREA
ON PROPERTY OF A.J. COX,
4 MILES SOUTHEAST OF SWITZER,
SPARTANBURG COUNTY, S.C.

SCALE IN FEET

Contour Interval 2ft.   Datum Assumed
Date of Mapping: October 23—November 5, 1936

LEGEND

Contour
Rim of gully
Drainage divide
Intermittent stream
Cross sections   2——2'

FIGURE 79.—Topographic map of the Cox's gully area.

77788°—39   (Face p. 116)

Map of Cox Gully, Spartanburg County, S.C.
(Drawn by Soil Conservation Service, 1930s)

Cox Gully

After lunch we drove south and west for the third stop of Terry's daylong Friends of the Pleistocene excursion. We pulled the van fleet into the small parking lot of the Switzer Church of God, established in 1937, just down the road from a historic Colonial home called the Price House. We were there to explore the final gully of the field trip.

The Price House was one of the county's early agricultural settlements, named after the Scotch-Irish settler family that built a tall, handsome brick manse in 1795. Though one of the first areas settled in the county, the area around the Price House was now sparsely peopled and mostly devoid of agriculture; the land was as gullied as any for miles and was given over now mostly to large hunt clubs with pine, white tail deer, and turkey the only crops. On the lonely twisting back roads like the one where we parked, an occasional mid-century modern ranch house squatted on a mowed half-acre lot. The area had been through a recent land grab, though, as several large carbon fiber plants purchased flat ridge-top land just off the interstate several miles north. Human occupation could be measured in layers, and in the early twenty-first century the agricultural layer had clearly given way once again to a manufacturing layer as the Piedmont's primary crop around the Price House. I said "once again" because the area's first textile mill had been established just a few miles downstream on the Tyger River in the early 1800s.

"I'll admit I don't know much about such things but isn't every church a church of God?" one of the scientists joked as he squeezed out of my van, although he quickly focused on the science again as Terry gathered everyone. Placing the church and cemetery as backdrop, he too tried to float a joke of his own: "Here we have some exposed granite outcrops," he said, pointing to the gravestones.

Terry gestured toward the woods and described gully number three. Cox Gully was one of the few sites in Spartanburg County that the soil men had explored in the 1930s and that was still the object of active research. Terry pointed to his oversized map. Behind the church, he explained, was an older roadbed probably dating back to Colonial days, but that old road had been crosscut by a lengthening arm of Cox Gully so severely that the road had to be moved.

As Terry explained the local gullying, I wandered the back edge of the crowd and listened to the side conversations bubbling up like springs everywhere: all the information Terry had presented so far on the other two stops had seeped into a dozen debates and discussions between colleagues. The further back from the front of the crowd you got the louder the conversations. If the Friends of the Pleistocene had been an army unit, it would have been close to mutiny at that moment. It was like that scene in *Monty Python's Life of Brian* in which the listeners at the rear of the Sermon on the Mount thought Jesus was talking about "cheese makers" rather than "peace makers."

I listened to the murmuring pods of scientists debating the definition of saprolite, the depth of weathered underlying bedrock, and whether the paradigm of the Piedmont had indeed shifted under their feet. One colleague whispered to an adjacent colleague an agitated question, "Couldn't these filled valleys be part of an ancient fluvial system?"

What had them so stirred up? In order to understand I had to go way back in time. Most of these scientists started the field trip considering the Piedmont one of most stable land surfaces on the planet. The tall mountains, then the rolling hills, had been ground down very gradually over eons by steady stream action. Of course, no matter when I want to begin it, the Piedmont story began way back in the basement of time. Half a billion years ago, Pangea was a supercontinent, a mashup; the future would unfold through waves of rifts, warps, and buckles. Crustal plates collide, mountains rise, an ancestral ocean opens, mountains erode, the ocean basin closes and opens again.

What stirred all the loud discussion at the back of the crowd was how, if Terry was right, the soil men had turned that stable Piedmont paradigm on its head. They had suggested that the Piedmont landscape was much more dynamic than anyone ever believed. In spite of the agitation in the ranks the field trip kept right on going. Time was Terry's enemy as the day was eroding fast and there were two more stops before supper. He was focusing mostly on the present or near-present on this stop—the historic road, the Price House and the ruined agricultural fields, and the work the geologists did to "treat" the existing gullies in the 1930s. "The agricultural potential of this watershed was destroyed by the early nineteenth century," Terry yelled. "I know we keep jumping back and forth in time. If you are confused, wave your arms." One guy held up both arms and shook them vigorously and everybody laughed, including Terry.

The spot of the Cox Gully was really special—in view of the multi-generational gully research done there in the 1930s up until 2000—but with the eighteenth-century Price House in the distance and the little white church, the cemetery, and the old road nearby, it began to take on more meaning. I guess you could say that my humanities gene had kicked in.

As Terry finally led the horde off down the road to enter Cox Gully, I conducted a quick walking survey of the grave markers in the little cemetery. There were two dozen graves with interments from 1938 until the present—Bishops, Teagues, Wards, Browns, Watsons, Gwinns, and Simmons, good English and Scotch-Irish names common to the Piedmont.

I wondered about the Brown who was buried there. Was the deceased related to me? The dark-stained, angular granite stone was shaped like a tablet and was one of the few in the cemetery with fresh flowers, purple tulips in a green urn. "Forever with the Lord," the epitaph stated across the bottom, obscured by the flowers' colorful vertical display.

I pushed into my own data and created my own stories, to go my own way. My people, my place, the element of time, the science behind the formation of gullies and the Piedmont land surface—I had lived with all these obsessions almost my entire intellectual life. I had always believed that understanding where you are helps you understand who you are. So for answers I had attached myself, as Terry had, to the ideas of dead people, a data set from the thirties, and a band of geoscience ghosts, and I listened for the insights that came from direct observation and experience. I wanted to notice everything and remember it all. But I knew memory wasn't the key to my life. Storytelling was. Story is what secures the insecure for me. Would these scientists formulate a new story about the Piedmont that would suffice? Terry had given them the clues he'd discovered in the scrapbook. Now it was up to them to put the pieces together.

I came back to the present and I caught up with the Friends of the Pleistocene and I noticed a tee shirt one student wore. He was a young Eargle, Ferguson, Eppes, or Richter. It said, "I am a geologist." Then I noticed the girl standing next to him. Hers said, "Make More Detours." The ghosts were talking to me through gravestones and tee shirt slogans.

Beauty Queen

When Mama was a teenager, she was beautiful—Lauren Bacall beautiful—with wavy dark hair, a big smile, and the kind of brown eyes a Camp Croft Army boy could easily fall into over the dinner table after church on Sunday or in a chance encounter in the downtown Army-Navy store where she later worked. I knew about her beauty not because I remembered it so much but because of several eight-by-ten, hand-tinted studio photos, something like a movie star leaves behind. There were multiple prints and poses, in several outfits, an unthinkable luxury for a mill family, though a reality because both my sister and I had the photos. Mama had little opportunity for most of her fully bloomed teenage years to turn her beauty to her advantage.

In 1925 our grandmother Hulda Bradley met Lon Brown, and they were married. They'd both been working at Beaumont Mill in Spartanburg. Mama was born at home in March of 1926. In the first photo Sandy has of Mama she's six months old—September of 1926. She has on a white dress and she sits outside in a rocking chair draped with two dark winter coats. She's barefooted. "The bottoms of her feet are clean, so she's not walking yet," Sandy pointed out. There is what looks like a birthmark on Mama's left cheek, and there's something stunned about the look on her face, as if the infant is staring out into the future and sees all the trouble like a flood rolling her way.

The next summer, 1927, Hulda was pregnant with Mama's sister Lottie. Lon had a car or borrowed one because they made a family trip up Highway 221 to Hillsville, Virginia, to a family reunion for the Mabes on the farm I'd once visited on my trip back from Virginia.

Mary Ellen Brown, Our Mother, in Photo Taken for
"Textiles Go to War" (Jack West, May 1943)

That summer in Hillsville, Lon began one of the central gullies of our family story that would wind and twist through the landscape for the next thirty-five years. Lon walked out and abandoned his pregnant wife Hulda and his young daughter, our mother Mary Ellen. He just disappeared. They wouldn't see him again for twenty years.

After her abandonment Hulda took Mama back to Spartanburg and moved in with her parents, John Simeon Bradley and Ella Mabe Bradley. Hulda stayed with her parents until she met and married Jim Norris in 1930, a man eighteen years her senior. Jim Norris had worked all over the region in textile mills—Belton, Fountain Inn, and Toxaway Mill in Anderson, until he was hired at Saxon Mills outside Spartanburg. Hulda had seven children by Jim Norris, including a set of twins.

Jim Norris was a loom fixer, important work consisting of setting up, adjusting, and repairing looms. He was a religious man, a churchgoer, and fiercely non-union. During the war he hauled soldiers in an old car from Camp Croft to church, then took them home to eat and flirt with the older girls. It was here Mama maybe first met soldiers. Maybe over Sunday dinner she met Gordon Cook, a paratrooper killed on D-Day. She always talked about the Yankee boy, whose picture she kept her whole life. She said he wanted to marry her.

Mama was nicknamed "Winnon," because the Norris twins couldn't pronounce Mary Ellen due to a speech impediment. They called her "Well-on," and it gradually changed into "Winnon." Lottie and all the half-siblings adopted the name.

Mama's stepfather Jim Norris was adamant about all the children going to the Free Will Baptist church. But Mama wanted to do other things. She dropped out of school in the eighth grade to work in a Saxon boarding house, and then she worked downtown at a drugstore lunch counter where she was fired for trying to organize the waitresses. Her stepfather Jim Norris was furious that she was fired, but her union grandfather approved. A decade earlier, in the Strike of '34, he'd wanted to beat up his son-in-law for crossing the picket line and would have liked to have killed him.

Mama was fifteen when the war started. Jim Norris mostly kept Mama's beauty hidden. She wasn't allowed to date or go to dances. She only saw a movie once as a teenager, and only saw it after her aunt snuck her into town. Things were so tense that at one point Mama and her sister Lottie left home and moved in with their grandparents, the Bradleys.

In 1943 Mama's stepfather Jim Norris died, and the pressure to be so righteous eased up, though there were other pressures. Later in life Mama talked a lot about the war, how hard it was with rationing. As the oldest child she had to work at the mill, so her mother, sister, and seven half-brothers and half-sisters could keep their company housing.

Mama always said Saxon Mill owner John Adger Law saw her in the spinning room and told her he was going to put her in the "Textiles Go to War" beauty contest with girls from twenty-five different county mills, and one of them would be crowned Textile Queen. Many decades later the local paper printed a black-and-white photo of Mama sitting in her favorite chair holding the fifty-year-old photo, so that it was possible to see who she was then and who she had become. Her gray hair was still the same length it was in the contest, and it still had the body it did when she was a young woman, but her fingers were twisted by arthritis. Her eyes were still kind and wide open enough to fall into, though framed by a cheap pair of reading glasses. The white blouse of the 1940s had been replaced by a dark jumper top bearing two hearts, one striped and one spotted, and a herd of tiny megafauna—a zebra, giraffe, and tiger. I think maybe she sewed this top herself.

For the contest, the mill bought Mama a nice dress and took her to Jack West's studio. West, a prominent photographer downtown, shot the portraits we still have. Before the contest a big car picked Mama up and drove her to town. She paraded in front of ten thousand people at Duncan Park that day. Zero Mostel, who trained at Camp Croft, was the master of ceremonies. Unless you are obsessed with obscure 1940s singers and comedians, you may not remember that Zero Mostel was best known for his role as Tevye on stage in

Fiddler on the Roof. Mama always spoke of him as if he were as famous as John Wayne.

"It was big just to get into town," Mama recalled in the newspaper article fifty years later. "I turned the wrong way and about walked off the stage." She came in second, but for runner-up they handed her a one-hundred-dollar war bond, the equivalent of fifteen hundred dollars today, and they put her picture in *Life*.

For me, Mama's life only began to come into sharp resolution about the time she appeared in *Life*. That event was like the pollen grains deposited in the gullies, something I could read and understand. The article revealed so much about the climate of Mama's early life. At that moment on that stage in 1943, it looked like Mama might take off. The photo session at Jack West's studio led to a job that got her out of the mill. The photographer owned the Army-Navy store downtown with a jewelry counter, and she liked working there. It also led to the family leaving Saxon, as there was nobody else to work in the mill.

The *Life* magazine in which Mama appeared came out on June 14, 1943. There was a high school graduate on the cover, and inside was a three-page spread called "Byrnes Goes Home: The 'Assistant President' Visits His South Carolina Neighbors and Talks About the War." The shiny magazine is almost seventy years old. In the story's lead photo United States Senator James F. "Jimmy" Byrnes sits with his arms crossed wearing a white suit, hat, and shoes in a large crowd at Duncan Park baseball stadium near downtown. His wife is next to him in a flowered dress and hat and dark gloves, and she looks a little bored. The next page shows Mama, one of six young women Byrnes might have been watching, walking proudly, a little tentatively, across the stage.

In '44 Mama left the mill behind, forged her freedom out of her stepfather Jim Norris's shadow, and finally went to work at the Army-Navy store downtown for Jack West, the man who had photographed her for the beauty contest. That was where Mama began to date soldiers from Camp Croft and dance at the clubs. Mama carried a copy of that *Life* article folded up in her purse until she died.

When she was elderly, I bought her a little tape player she could keep beside her easy chair. Her favorite cassette she wore out from rewinding was Bob Seger's "Against the Wind." Her favorite line from it was, "I wish I didn't know now what I didn't know then." I often wondered if it was meeting Sandy's father she was thinking about when she played that song over and over.

Legacy

The simple explanation for why Terry led me on another excursion into Spartanburg County is to extract a recently inserted aluminum pipe that he hoped would reveal "a stratified soil profile/core sample all the way to bedrock." With this data from stream level, Terry's contemporary soil profile would be complete all the way across a small stream drainage he was studying, an example of classic Piedmont geography, "deeply weathered, soils eroded so severely in the last two hundred years that essentially all the productivity has been washed away."

Near my foot, the shallow, muddy ruts of a four-wheeler trail eroded out a sloping, agreeable approach to Big Ferguson Creek (no relation), four hundred feet upstream from the creek's confluence with the South Tyger River. The recent four-wheeler ruts did not appear on Terry's high-tech LIDAR ("Light Detection and Ranging"), a high-resolution mapping technique that Terry often consulted in our preparation for fieldwork to identify intriguing features in a landscape. Terry's LIDAR image was so dense with shadowing that the black and tan surface looked like someone had scratched it with a stylus. The Tyger River meandered southeast and wiggled through flattened basins defined by the river's bumper car battles with the hills over the millennia. For our excursion we'd parked the departmental SUV on the old Gap Creek Road, a thoroughfare you can see very clearly on the LIDAR as a snaky scar intersecting the durable, hard edge of the modern highway.

I followed Terry and Ben Thomas, Terry's former student, down the muddy four-wheeler trail to the edge of the creek. Ben was on summer break. Dressed in tan cargo shorts, a college sorority weekend tee shirt, and a cap, Ben was one in a long line of Terry's undergraduate collaborators. Ben had been an excellent student as an

Ben Thomas Extracting Legacy Sediments, Big Ferguson Creek
(John Lane, 2016)

undergraduate. Then he persisted with good humor through two summers of long hours with Terry, gathering data from Big Ferguson Creek for his senior environmental studies capstone, and teasing out a manageable piece of a complex local landscape puzzle, a small enough slice of research to put his name on a scientific poster at a professional meeting. Ben hoped to go to graduate school in geography after a gap year working over in Greenville.

Besides Terry and Ben, I was accompanied into the field by a whole cast of dead men—scientists mostly—who spent time here in or near Spartanburg County in the 1930s and 1940s when this place was one of the epicenters of federal soil research through the Soil Conservation Service. This area of the South was the one most impacted by soil erosion in the whole region. Two hundred years of logging and farming had destroyed almost all of the vital capacity of Piedmont soils. Nineteenth-century and twentieth-century tenant farmers and sharecroppers grew fields of cotton, and after two centuries of farming, the soils disappeared down the slopes and the streams became clogged with silt "legacy sediments," referring to clay, silt, and sand washed off the uplands and deposited in the bottoms.

As the soils moved downslope regional farming mostly collapsed as a viable livelihood and industry. Over time, the Piedmont lost more than a foot of topsoil. By the 1930s there was a war being waged against this soil erosion, and its main battlefront was the South Carolina Piedmont. The work done here by engineers and scientists was the front line for understanding and attempting to correct the issue. Hugh Hammond Bennett, the first director of the Soil Conservation Service, was determined to solve the problem of gullying, return the land to fertility, and assure prosperity to southern upcountry farmers; hence great effort went into filling in gullies, terracing land, and pondering soil erosion. Bennett worked heroically at that—so did an army of engineers, agents, and laborers. University-trained scientists with curious minds had an almost endless supply of labor provided by Civilian Conservation Corps camps of the 1930s. Before these Depression-era researchers could publish all their findings, World War II shifted all their sharp minds to food and war production, and local Piedmont data disappeared into the National Archives.

As we walked into the woods at Big Ferguson Creek, Terry reminded me that there are many forces at work in the Upstate, forces of dynamic change. I remembered John Harrington's advice to me, "Life is about doing things, Lad." So I walked onward with Terry. As we moved down toward Big Ferguson Creek, memories of my three geology classes washed over me like a rainstorm. The details of Harrington's field trips, the books he wrote, our conversations about poetry and geology, and the last visit I had with him before he died soaked me to the bone.

Ben had brought an extension ladder and once we reached the creek, he climbed down and held the aluminum ladder so Terry and I could descend. I looked around before following. Big Ferguson Creek was sharply entrenched about eight feet below me, and the stream itself ran in a shallow wash through the bottom of the trench. The water was slightly tinted, and in the angled sunlight that reached it through the trees on the ridge, the flow was both green and brown, depending on how the sun hit it. There was something always murky and sullied about a Piedmont stream, especially if it hasn't rained for weeks. This was not a place I would want to swim, even on a hot day like that.

In hot weather and in cold, I loved being in the Piedmont woods as much as any hunter or timber cruiser. And I loved noticing creatures like the assassin bug on the lip of the creek bank and the summer tanager singing above in the hardwoods. But Terry had invited me not only to reflect but to assist. The ladder sat parallel to a vertical trench cut back into the creek bank. At first glance it looked like a narrow, excavated chute of mud descending to creek level shaved off with a shovel blade from root-clogged top layer to a layer of grey clay at the bottom saturated with water. There were three or four flags inserted along the trench, demarcating important transitions. I knew this to be another "soil profile," like Richter had scraped on the first gully wall in the Friends of the Pleistocene field trip.

I asked if the depth of the channel was unusual, and Terry explained that the entrenchment was consistent with that of other streams in the area. "The sediment down at the surface of the stream dates to about 1300 AD, and then there's about a foot of deposition from 1300 AD until the 1700s," Terry explained, sweeping his hand over the surface of the soil profile below me in the steep riverbank. "And then the upper seven feet you're standing on was deposited since the mid-1700s, most since the 1870s."

Before European settlement began (around the 1760s in this watershed), dams diverting water to the numerous grist mills had a significant impact on stream profiles as well. Terry pointed out that, in spite of the impact of mill dams, many other elements contributed to the distribution of these profound loads of "human-sponsored sediment." Erosion from farming, Terry explained, is "an interesting sort of marker most folks don't usually think about."

I looked across Terry's research basin and saw nothing spectacular or unusual, nothing in my eyes that would be worth multiple research careers. Just Piedmont bottomland. Before I took Harrington's geology classes it would never have occurred to me to think of these places as dynamic, like layer cakes of sediment building up flood by flood over time. But that was what Terry was explaining, and it is what makes this place so special. This was where some of the initial research was completed that helped to explain the dynamics of stream flow and erosion in the Piedmont, that helped to pinpoint for researchers what had gone so terribly wrong with farming to bring on such extreme erosion in the uplands and burial of the bottomlands.

The pipe that Terry and Ben were trying to extract was stuck. They broke off the handle of the instrument used to extract sediment samples on an earlier expedition to recover the core, so we stood on the sand bar in the creek, Ben digging around the pipe stuck in the muck and Terry drilling through the tubing with a battery drill. Next Terry attached a rebar handle through the holes and we all three yanked like hell.

Terry and Ben had put in the pipe so they could sample sediment below the 1300 AD level to bedrock. Terry never failed to make a corny joke when there was an opportunity and slipped one in as we jerked on the pipe: "As an archaeologist I'm always looking for buried deposits."

Terry and Ben wanted the sample so they could send it to a lab for dating. They didn't know exactly how old this deposit was; they'd sampled deposits from elsewhere in the county and they'd all been what Terry called "carbon dead," meaning they were too old (over forty-five thousand years) to be dated with radiocarbon techniques. "So, we don't know yet if this buried organic deposit is Holocene or older." Forced to speculate, Terry said he thought the bottom of the sample would likely be less than fourteen thousand years old, placing it "after the Holocene-Pleistocene boundary, or the last Ice Age."

The three of us stood looking at the stuck pipe, and spirits started talking to me—the spirits of landforms, of epochs, of the people who taught me like John Harrington, of the dead people who had worked the land like my own family, and of those who had studied the land. Even the short, mild epoch called the Holocene is a ghost now, a period that always animated my six-decades-old imagination. Thinking about the Holocene was the way I learned to understand how humans had lived in this region for the past fourteen thousand years, a gift epoch now receding into the academic past. Remember me, the Holocene seemed to be saying, like Hamlet's ghost, as the new geologic epoch, called the Anthropocene, known as the period during which we humans have been the dominant force in nature, strutted and fretted upon the stage.

Here it was becoming obvious how much I was a poet informed by science, an interloper content to sample someone else's fieldwork. My reflections were directed at gathering types of data that were never recorded in field notebooks. My data was personal, not abstracted quite so much as numbers and models tended to do. I utilized the tool of language as my trowel—images, metaphor, story, all shaping my monograph of dream landscapes. *"Just get it down and then get it right, cobble together this story, and let someone else judge it and find its value,"* I wrote in my field notebook. I was fascinated by the pieces of this story—the personalities, the data, the element of deep time, the science behind the formation of gullies and the Piedmont land surface—because I have always believed that understanding where I am helps me understand who I am. But even in the face of such compelling science I couldn't shelve my thoughts about family. No one I was related to looked to this land for anything besides sustenance and support. There was no army of CCC workers to help my great-great-grandfather C. C. Bradley plow and plant the Piedmont fields he rented. But for the moment, in the field with Terry, I took my place among the intellectual speculators as I had been trained, and I attached myself, as Terry had, to a data set from the 1930s, a band of scientists, and the insights that come not from memory but from direct observation. *"Lord, they say soil envelopes the earth's body like a skin. But I say no. Soil isn't a skin. Soil is minerals, rock pulverized by time. I say it is our body."*

We tugged the stubborn pipe until it popped out. I walked away muddy as any sharecropper, inspired, and very satisfied. As I stood in the trench of the creek, deep time cascaded around me again as it once did in college, spiraling back toward the unsettled regions within which geologists, archaeologists, and soil scientists moved with ease. Deep time was manageable for a moment—in the flood plain and the creek that cuts through it. Time filled up the landscape bowl. It radiated outward in what I'd heard Terry call "stratification," sediment laid down as sheets of time, eroded soil transported from upstream. "The legacy sediments" were falling out over this small creek valley in silt layers, maybe one centimeter a year on average through historic times, maybe less down below at the horizon Terry called "the pre-settlement surface." How much could come of such explorations of land and life?

Mary Ellen Brown, Our Mother, Second from Right,
with Family Members, Irwin Avenue, Spartanburg, S.C.
(Photographer Unknown, 1944)

Irwin Avenue

It was hot as hell, midday, stark sun, blue skies, when I parked at Dee-Traxx, a rundown convenience store with a cool name, hard up against a railroad crossing on the rubble-strewn south side of Spartanburg. I was on a mission to peg some of the mystery years of our family's life before I was born not just to stories and photos, but to another place, a patch of real soil. I'd invited Sandy and she was on the way. I wanted, finally, to put down the roots of my imagination into the loam of our family's comings and goings. I knew Dee-Traxx, had passed it a thousand times. The store had been an icon of this dilapidated area for at least thirty years—the pantry in a food desert for the poor who lived in frame houses left over from a hosiery mill that used to operate nearby. Dee-Traxx had colonized this blinking light crossroads. The corner could have been in any former textile area in Spartanburg, downbound economically for decades, a refuge for those—some white, some Black—who couldn't afford to settle anywhere else. I felt an affinity for them all. These were the places I lived as a child, and because our family lived in places like this, I could claim them. Around me were the problems that I had growing up—how to eat well, where to live, how to survive.

The day was too hot for me to sit in my truck, even with the windows down, so I slipped out, crossed the road to the new bridge constructed to span Fairforest Creek, which drained the whole west side of Spartanburg, and looked down into the shallow waters. I looked upstream and saw the creek's shoals created entirely by busted bottles, rusted beams, and broken concrete, an urban stream carrying on through the rubble of settlement to the Atlantic two hundred miles away.

The bridge had opened three days earlier. It took a year to build, and the owner of Dee-Traxx complained publicly in the local paper that 80 percent of his business fell away when the bridge closed. Now it was open again, and the cars flowed freely in and out of the Dee-Traxx eddy, pumping gas, buying beer.

Sandy parked along the road shoulder next to Dee-Traxx. I waved and she slipped through the traffic to join me on the bridge. "The house was in that bamboo." Sandy pointed down next to the creek. There is not a scrap of the house left now. I looked hard for signs, but my gaze stalled at the green curtain shading the trashy creek. If anything was left of the house in the bamboo patch, we'd have to wait until winter to place our feet on solid family ground. It was rich with possibility though. When our people lived here briefly in the 1940s, the creekside view was probably a little more pleasant, a little bit more natural, especially for the kids. In our family's brief years there by Fairforest Creek, grandmother Hulda continued to raise five Norris kids, twelve or under, playing in the yard—Jim, J. C., Libby, the twins, Bobby and Billy. I'm sure they would have liked the flowing water in the creek behind the house.

The downtown airport on the ridge just up the hill was later a hub for the corporate jet traffic coming in and out of town, but during the war it was a military air strip. Mama would visit with her Uncle Lum, a mechanic at the airport and in the Civil Air Patrol. He took her aloft once, and she circled the city and looked down at her house from above. Lum did loops and stalls and scared Mama so bad she never flew again.

That year, there was also the Army captain who borrowed a Jeep and drove her to the end of the runway to sit for hours, talk, and watch the planes land. "Johnny, that man never tried to kiss me in all that time," she once said. "Do you think he was gay?"

Our grandmother owned this Irwin Avenue house four years after they left Saxon. There were mysteries about that time that even Sandy with all her genealogical skills will never solve, but she told me what she knew.

"Why didn't Mama stay at the mill?" I asked Sandy. "She must have felt like a celebrity after coming so close to winning that beauty contest."

"You can't live in mill housing if there is no member of the family employed." Sandy explained. So our grandmother bought a house across town from Saxon on Irwin Avenue. "She bought it in October of '43 for $1,500, likely with insurance money from Jim Norris's death."

Hulda moved her sprawling family of nine into the four rooms of the Irwin Avenue house. In a photo of the house Sandy showed me from that year, there was no underpinning, and it was sided with wood and in need of paint. There was a porch swing, and in the distance the countryside was open except for a small mill across the street.

Soon after the family moved in, Hulda married a third time. Sandy told me that this new husband was a man named Robert Lawrence Harvey, who came to Spartanburg from Tennessee, possibly for Camp Croft, and he had a small son. "Harvey moved in with them, and then soon after, he told Granny he was going to Tennessee. Then next thing they knew, Harvey sent money to put his son on a bus and that's the last they heard from him."

It was a little over a year after the move to Irwin Avenue that Mama met Sandy's father, Pvt. William Crawford Alverson. He was from up in Inman, "peach country," in the rolling Piedmont hills, and his family called him W. C. He was home on leave in December 1945 and in town that day with some of his military buddies. They came to the Army-Navy store where Mama worked and stood near the store's jewelry counter joking. Finally, the young man asked to see a diamond ring and said to Mama, "You're going to marry me." A photo of Sandy's father from his army years shows W. C. as handsome, blue eyed, scrub faced, and blonde haired. But there was something else about him. Too full of himself? A mama's boy? He had all he needed. He'd survived the war. He was back home. He was with his buddies, laughing at whatever they laughed about. What he thought he needed was this beautiful shy girl, a peach just ripe for the picking. Maybe that meeting was when it all really began. Mama meeting W. C. They married. That's all Sandy knew. Was there a courtship? One day Mama was working in a jewelry store, and the next she was married to W. C. Alverson and moving from Irwin Avenue to a peach farm up in Inman. "When he took her home to Inman, Mama claimed W. C.'s mother, Martha 'Mattie' Williams-McClure-Alverson, was not pleased," Sandy explained. "Mama thought, that W. C.'s mother looked down on her because her family was cotton mill workers, 'lintheads,' as some called them. It wasn't until much later, while researching the Bradley family line, that I stumbled upon maybe the real reason."

Mama moved into W. C.'s house with his mother and three half-sisters. His father was already dead. "After Mama moved up there, things went bad," Sandy explained.

We walked back across the road, leaned against the vehicles, and continued to talk. "I realized one of the farms the Bradleys rented once had to be where Mattie Alverson, my grandmother, had once lived," Sandy continued. "Mattie's family ties were from Cleveland, Polk, and Spartanburg Counties. She had lived all her life in those counties. Mr. Williams, her father, had been a preacher and traveled all over those areas also. I'm sure Mattie would have heard the gossip about the Bradleys' questionable ethnic roots. Did W. C.'s mother realize Mama was a descendant of the Bradleys, whose blood line was questionable? I have often wondered if that was the reason she was not welcoming to her son's new wife."

Sandy had heard another story from a woman near the area where the Bradleys lived on Island Ford Road: "The woman remembered that a Bradley family was refused admittance to the Harris School because it was rumored the children were part Black."

Sandy found out later, via DNA and contact with descendants, that the family was that of a distant cousin. "It seemed the deeper the research, the more conflict I found," Sandy said. "Another distant cousin asked after an interview, had I heard of the Black blood in the Bradleys? Yes, it has been mentioned, I responded. Of course, many of the family members have insisted over the years that the Bradleys had Indian blood, and a few were even embarrassed by that possibility. If I ever hinted that there was only a small percentage of Native

American, but a larger percentage of African, they would suggest it had to be wrong. It seems that all the people that I came in contact with during my research were told the same thing: the Bradleys had Indian in their roots and not to ask too many questions."

Somewhere in the past generation—at least for me—questions about identity and origins fell away, or more likely they never surfaced at all, but I could not ignore that they mattered more to the generations before me. What Sandy has called "the gossip" about my second-great-grandfather Bradley's genetic makeup may have contributed to Mama's instability. Getting thrown out of your mother-in-law's house isn't something you get over quickly. It certainly contributed to how my beloved sister viewed herself and her place in the world. She's told me that the one time Mama took her up to Inman to visit her grandmother Alverson, there was a palpable sense that neither of them was welcome.

But it was not only W. C. Alverson's mother that was the problem in our Mama's first marriage. Sandy recounted a few more of the stories of Mama's terrible first marriage. Soon after Mama moved in, W. C. picked up an old girlfriend and drove past the house so Mama could see. They argued about it. Mama got mad, went to town. When she came back, her clothes had been thrown out in the road. W. C. went back to Germany, and Mama went back to Granny's down on Irwin Avenue. One of Mama's younger sisters once showed Sandy a photo from Irwin Avenue taken when their sister Lottie got married in October of 1946. "See that?" our aunt asked. "Your Mama was already pregnant."

And Lon Brown? "By the time Mama met W. C. Alverson, Lon Brown had been gone and assumed dead for twenty years," Sandy told me. Was he really dead? Mama wrote the Browns to find out. Lon Brown's niece responded and said, no, Lon Brown was not dead after all. He was alive and living in Lantana, Florida. Then either Mama or Granny wrote to Lon Brown and undoubtedly, he asked if they would come and visit. That summer they went to Lantana the first time. They took the train. It must have been quite a sight when Lon Brown met the whole family at the train station.

"They didn't stay long that first time. What was the purpose of this trip?" I asked.

"Hulda seemed to be going down to reacquaint herself with Lon Brown, the father of two of her nine children, and Mama and Lottie went down to meet their father for the first time. Mama was just a baby when Lon Brown left, and he'd been gone for months when Lottie was born. I wish I'd been able to ask Lon Brown about his motives, but he probably would have flimflammed his way to an answer," Sandy responded.

The family came back to Spartanburg after that first trip to Lantana, and later went back and ended up staying, either in Lantana or on Anastasia Island, where Lon Brown had bought a lot. It was obvious that Lon Brown convinced Hulda that they should get back together.

Mama must have felt comfortable with Lon Brown, as hard as that is to believe. Sandy said Mama once told her Lottie "hated Lon Brown's guts," but you did not get that feeling from Mama.

Sandy and I stood in the heat and looked across the road at the site of the vanished Irwin Avenue house. A few years earlier Sandy had been on the internet searching for genealogical information and discovered that our family river was even muddier than she knew. Hulda had married yet another man while she was down in Florida—Sherman Odell Carter. Their marriage was January 10, 1947 in Lee County, Florida. Hulda was thirty-eight and Carter was forty-three. The marriage lasted a year. That relationship was a complete mystery except for the papers Sandy discovered—the marriage license and divorce papers from 1948. One of our aunts remembered Sherman Carter: "She was friendly with him, but I didn't know they had actually married."

What was our grandmama doing? It seemed impossible to me to sort all the relationships out. Was she a fool for love? Was it transactional? I knew in those days a marriage was sometimes one of the only ways for a single woman with children to feed them. Then I thought of my own long series of monogamous relationships, my brief chaotic marriage in my twenties, and how only in my forties I had found my way to a secure union that is now two decades old.

Sandy reminded me, "Family stories are thick from those years, but the material evidence is scant."

There was one letter from Lon Brown's niece to Hulda written in September of '47 after they went down to Florida to see him. It was chatty, but she reminded Lon Brown's ex-wife, "He isn't like his parents. He sure does drink—bad." Then there was one from Lon Brown to Hulda—written in pencil, almost faded to white. They'd already been to Florida to visit. Lon Brown was persuasive. He pleaded for them all to come down and live:

My dear wife and all Will rite you and hope you got home all OK. Sure did hate to see you go And hope you git there alright and I move down to the place today. Sure do miss you here and want you to come on back soon as you can for this is lonesome hear all I feel all alone and will be lonesome until you all git hear with me. And be glad when all of us come down hear and I will get us a box at the post office and have to hear from you all soon. And I will be waiting for you all. I remain your husband and dad

Sandy had brought several other photos with her, and we spread them out on the hood of her car and looked at them there in the heat. "These were from Florida," she explained. "This one was taken on Anastasia Island. It's a wide shot of the whole yard."

The photo was posed and showed Lon Brown and his oldest daughter, Mama, leaning against a large palm tree with sand beneath them. Lon Brown had one hand in his left pocket and the other arm around Mama with his outstretched fingers resting on the wrist of her arm, which she held over her chest and striped top. In her other hand she dangled a cigarette, the first hint of the habit that she wouldn't shake before her life ended. Mama was young and looked hopeful, smiling, and beautiful, just as she did in the "Textiles Go to War" beauty contest photos three years earlier.

When I first saw these photos I was taken by how slender Mama was, and how her thick hair fell to her shoulders. Maybe she thought her future was wide open to the horizon. The war had ended. Florida was booming. There seemed to be cash and stability. It was obvious that the Anastasia Island house was on the beach. Was the house Lon Brown's? Did Mama arrive from abject poverty in Spartanburg, with her year-old girl-child, only to find Lon Brown, who abandoned them twenty years earlier, living the Florida dream? This would make sense if it was indeed the second time they visited, when Mama always said her father had bought land on Anastasia Island, and could have been rich from it had he kept it, which might explain the waterfront. Sandy said the property records showed he only owned a single lot—not the basis for the riches Mama always prophesized.

"These other photos were taken in Florida too," Sandy explained.

In another photo, Mama's sister Lottie sat on the front steps with her arms crossed, in shorts with a tube top and tan lines over each shoulder; her new husband Norman sat behind her, legs wide, hands resting on his knees in a white sagging sleeveless tee. Grandfather Lon Brown sat behind them next to a tropical plant, in a white shirt and long pants, holding a dog with Yoda ears. Sandy was the shirtless bronze child balancing the composition on the right.

Lon Brown was darkly tanned too, and he wore the same white shirt in all four photos. In three of the others Mama was there; in two she wore a white tee shirt and a dark brimmed hat (the photos were black and white) with her hair up. In the first she held a hydraulic silver spray paint gun (Lon Brown was a house painter by trade) and struck a hipshot pose, like a model; she pointed at an upright kitchen chair. In the second, they had turned the chair over and continued to paint, and Lon Brown pointed at a spot Mama had missed. Mama had penciled across the bottom of this one, "Me & Daddy."

C. Horizon

The lowermost zone, consisting mainly of unconsolidated rock fragments. This horizon is associated with what is called weathered "parent rock."

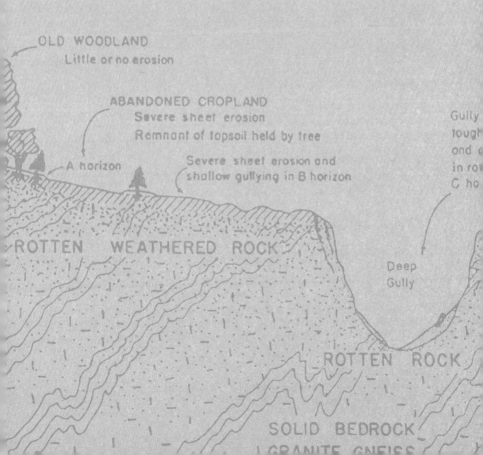

OLD WOODLAND
Little or no erosion

ABANDONED CROPLAND
Severe sheet erosion
Remnant of topsoil held by tree

A horizon

Severe sheet erosion and
shallow gullying in B horizon

Gully
tough
and
in ro
C ho

ROTTEN WEATHERED ROCK

Deep
Gully

ROTTEN ROCK

SOLID BEDROCK
GRANITE GNEISS

Columbus Christopher Bradley (Front Row Center with Hat)
and Three Generations of Family, Taken near Fingerville, Spartanburg
County, S.C. (Photographer Unknown, ca. 1908)

Rediscovering the Bradleys

A few weeks later I was back in the field with Terry. We took a wandering scouting trip north in the county to further Terry's gully research. He wanted to visit the area that the geographer Carl O. Sauer had scouted in the 1930s. I was back in science mode too, or so I thought. I had felt, after the visit to Dee-Traxx and the painful stories about Sandy's father, that maybe it was time to lay family history aside for a little while. The plan was for Terry and me to stop at the crossroads of Highway 11 and the Spartanburg Road, a wide spot long known as Fingerville, named not for the digital shape of its town layout, but for early textile pioneer Joseph Finger who opened a cotton mill here in 1849 on the North Pacolet River. There, near the Fingerville crossroads, was the site of one of the gullies that Sauer visited.

Carl O. Sauer made several visits to Spartanburg County in the company of Soil Conservation Service men. Some of Sauer's ideas about land and life were formed in the South Carolina Piedmont along Highway 11. As a powerful consultant, Sauer had seeded the SCS with like-minded thinkers, several of them his graduate students, bright young men Sauer turned loose on Spartanburg County, who were part of the Climatic and Physiographic Division, part of the pure research arm of the SCS. Sauer's student Charles Warren Thornthwaite was named director of the Climatic and Physiographic Division, and he was free to direct the study of soil and sedimentation that was not tied directly to what today would be called "agricultural extension." In other words, the work of Thornthwaite and others wasn't directly applied to alleviating the dramatic gullying of Spartanburg County, which Hugh Hammond Bennett, the head of the SCS, had called soil erosion, "a national menace."

Sauer came to the South to serve as an active consultant for the scs. In the summer of 1936 he took a field trip out into the county with other scientists, including Andy Ireland and Stewart Sharpe. In an interview Terry found that Sharpe gave in 1991, the old researcher remembered that they got started once Sauer came east. They spent a couple of weeks with Sauer in the Piedmont, and Sauer developed an ambitious research agenda, which he outlined in his report about the trip, suggesting they study gully formation and erosion. He also wanted "erosion history" research to elucidate what human practices had contributed to erosion or possibly limited it. There was also a plan to pursue research into the problem of the Piedmont's filled valleys. Sharpe said being in the field with him was like a graduate seminar. Sharpe said Sauer loved graveyards. He even visited the [Catawba] Indian reservation and talked to chief Blue. "Everything was grist to Sauer's mill."

"Sauer always stirred it up," Sharpe later remembered. While he was in Spartanburg, Sauer went up to a meeting in Chapel Hill and told them they should never have grown cotton in the Piedmont. "Sauer didn't clear that with scs headquarters."

Little was known at that point about hydrology and how it impacted soils. Many environmental historians consider Sauer on par with Aldo Leopold as a popularizer of thinking about landscapes. Since 1923 Sauer had been a professor of geography at UC–Berkeley, but he also had become a powerful mentor, researcher, and consultant, with far-reaching affiliations in geography circles and beyond. To many who both admired him and criticized him, he was known as "the Great God from beyond the Sierras." Sauer was one of two geographers at the time ever elected to the Academy of Science. In the 1930s Sauer was known much more widely as a geomorphologist, a geologist interested in the physical features of the surface of the earth and how they are expressive of the underlying geology.

In the 1970s when I began to write, any poet interested in landscape read Carl O. Sauer. As a student I discovered references to Sauer in the work of Charles Olson and Gary Snyder, two poets I was reading back then. When I moved to Port Townsend, Washington, in 1979, I was thrust into bioregionalism, an intellectual back-to-the-land movement; at the insistence of several West Coast poets a paper-back of *Land and Life* (1969) was one of the first books I purchased and added to my personal library. I read Sauer, far from home, and far from the gullied, red clay Piedmont that was part of the history of both Sauer and me.

Land and Life was a kind of poetry. Like the poetry I then preferred by poets like Gary Snyder, the collection was hard edged, aphoristic, full of natural history observation, deeply researched, with academic insight about the role of human beings in the environment. Sauer's studies ranged from the natural conditions of pioneer life to a piece that was the favorite among the poets like Olson and Snyder—"The Morphology of Landscape," first published in 1925. "The facts of geography are place facts," Sauer wrote. "The facts of history are time facts . . . An ordered presentation of the landscapes of the earth is a formable undertaking." When I read this in my twenties I automatically transferred Sauer's ideas to my own. There were also facts of the self and of the inner life, and as a poet I was determined to write them down directly. I wanted to create my own morphology, a study of the form and relationship of my inner and outer self.

Though known widely as a geographer, Sauer was also one of the original ecological thinkers too. He saw human life, the larger biome, the geomorphology that supports us, even the chemistry, as all one. Once I had read Sauer, it didn't take me long to apply his ideas about landscape to my own personal Piedmont. His thinking dovetailed nicely with what I had already learned in college from Harrington. If Harrington had successfully converted me to the idea of "deep time," it was Sauer who filled in the foreground and helped me to see the cultural landscape. When I returned to the South in the early 1980s, I realized I was seeing the land through Sauer's eyes as well as Harrington's. I had developed binocular vision. I loved the way Sauer focused observers on "the content of a landscape," its associations, both natural and cultural, in both time and space.

This interest in geography and landscape was one of the central themes of my early poetry, in addition to family. To me they seemed natural partners for exploring the interior world. Poetry engaged me early on for its ability to express emotion and encapsulate deep feeling in single images. Those images were often best found in the natural world.

I have often wondered why I loved formal prose writing and the comfort of clear theses, yet headed in the direction of poetry. In my poems I trust images to say what I want to say, and in my stories I have a wandering tone reminiscent of an ancient storyteller. The easy answer is that I come from a long line of storytellers, my mother foremost among them. A more complex answer might be that after Daddy's death I never had a father figure in the house. I never had a resident male to center my personal story, to give me a primary premise, an example to look up to regarding what might be maintained or proved true enough to matter.

If framed as a poem or a story, my family life might be looked at as a failed essay, a prose project with a first draft that started out a mess—a suicide father and an absentee mother—with the narrator wandering among too many options. Over time, the wandering itself became the thesis.

Thesis comes from the Greek, "to place or propose." I have always placed myself in motion. Like Satchel Paige, I didn't often look back because I knew something might be gaining on me.

The best way to throw off the hounds is to cross and recross the creek, and poetry is a way both to throw off the hounds and pet them at the same time. It would be easy to say that "the hounds" are bouts of depression, or the fear of my father's suicide, but I don't think it's that easy. I have lived a fairly depression-free life, and at least since high school, I have not avoided facing Daddy's early physical exit from my life. I have written about my father in essays and poems. Many of my best-known poems, written about the time that I reached the age that he reached when he took his own life (44), are stories that contain his ghost. In these poems my father is as real as he can be. His ghost returns often in everything I do, including the writing of this story.

When we arrived in Fingerville, Terry pulled over and displayed a plat he had brought along. His goal was to locate one of the first gullies where Sauer and some of his team had noted the buried organic deposits in Spartanburg. The nicely drawn plat was marked "Alverson." There was a small black square indicating "the Alverson farmhouse," one of only two structures in the 1930s study area. I felt a little stunned. Alverson? It looked like I couldn't leave our family stories behind after all. I recalled Mama's first brief marriage soon after World War II. I imagined the child who resulted in their tumultuous encounter and bonding at the end of World War II. That child was Sandy. The family of Sandy's father had an association with the northern end of the county—their involvement with peach farming. While pregnant, Mama stayed a few months on a peach farm before her new husband, W. C. Alverson, returned to Germany as part of the occupation force. Could that be the farmhouse? Could I have a personal connection to this very gully? Could this be the Alverson house where Mama had stayed?

I tried to focus on the gully, a dotted line shaped like a worm bending back northwest. On the plat the gully's southwestern tail graded into the head of Obed Creek, a small tributary of the North Pacolet River. "This is one of the first gullies where Sauer and Ireland found the buried organic deposits," Terry narrated. I looked down into the real gully and saw it was full of dead kudzu. It would be difficult to find the bottom, much less the buried organic deposits hidden within. Obviously, the descent into the gully was something for another excursion.

The land to the West was higher, and after we loaded back into Terry's truck, we turned off Highway 11 onto a parallel gravel road. We drove to where the Alverson house sat on the ridge, which topped out a few hundred yards to the West. The house was a gingerbread Victorian, still occupied after all these years. We parked and Terry walked to the door. No one answered. There in the yard of the old farmhouse I experienced the first mystical coincidence of the day. I looked at the plat again.

When we were back in the truck I sent Sandy a picture of the old Alverson farmhouse and the plat of the Alverson farm. My sister texted back pretty quickly—"I believe this is a photo of Doctor Franklin Alverson's house. He's a third cousin of my father. He was just named Doctor. He was a farmer, not a doctor."

I texted Sandy back, asking about Mama's connection. In the meantime, Sandy texted again to tell me that not only did I have a once-removed connection to the Alverson farm, but even stranger, our great-great-grandfather Columbus Christopher Bradley had lived and farmed near there as well in 1920, just over a decade and a half before Sauer and his soil men came through on their field trip.

"What?"

"He died at the Johnson farm just down the road."

Once the exchanges registered, I texted Sandy back. "I'll call when I get back to town." I took a deep breath to help process what Sandy had just told me. To Terry I might have looked like I'd had a visitation, which in a way I had experienced.

"My sister says our genetic ancestors were tenant farmers who lived and farmed near here," I said. "I'm implicated directly in the destruction of the Piedmont's landscape through erosion over two centuries."

And then I laid it out for him with a little more detail. First, Mama's people, the Bradleys—maybe Black, maybe white, or a little of both, as my sister's genealogical research shows—worked for the iron industry for multiple generations at High Shoals up Highway 221 in Rutherford County, North Carolina, and then when that industry failed, they began farming. Then in the 1870s, my people escaped down Highway 221 into the upper Piedmont and farmed there for several decades. Then as the farming failed, many of them moved on down 221 into Spartanburg to work the textile mills.

"That's it in a nutshell," I said.

The Alversons lasted longer than the Bradleys in agriculture, and they had some standing in the community. By the time Carl Sauer and his team showed up on this farm, the Alversons were prosperous, and became even more so, moving from cotton to peaches. Peaches stayed viable into the 1980s in Spartanburg County. Peach orchards sprawled along the ridge tops and were fitted in around the gullies. But the fickle Piedmont weather almost doomed them in the end.

"I don't care what the back-to-the-land advocates say," Terry continued as we headed back to Spartanburg. "We can't live off this land. The soils aren't productive anymore. It will never recover."

"Couldn't we just keep using artificial fertilizer?"

"You can make grass grow on a concrete block, but what about the broader scale of the landscape? Phosphorous, nitrogen, the destruction of streams and habitats by runoff."

"So this is why so many left and went to the mills in those decades?" I asked.

"Exactly. Your great-great-grandfather couldn't have kept farming. Agriculture in the Piedmont was over by the time he died. Your great-great-grandfather was an erosion refugee," Terry said.

"*Grapes of Wrath* come to Spartanburg."

"Yes."

And I wasn't exaggerating. To Hugh Hammond Bennett these gullies were just like the Dust Bowl.

"You know, Terry," I said. "This is no longer an abstract lab problem like Harrington might have formulated for a geology lab. This is personal."

Johnny Lane and Paula in Pinebluff, N.C. (Mary Ellen Brown Lane, Easter 1955)

Sandy Ground

My sister drove us the old way to Pinebluff, three hours east from Spartanburg on US Highway 74. Mama made many trips after we left Southern Pines when Daddy died. Until we were older we always came with her. "This is the way Mama would have come in the '60s," Sandy reflected as we rolled along.

Sandy's a good driver, but I picked up some of Mama's nervousness about highways and travel. As Sandy switched lanes on busy downtown Independence Boulevard she noticed I looked stressed. "Mama always panicked in Charlotte," Sandy remembered. "That's why we left in the middle of the night."

"I inherited that," I said.

"Me, I'm different." Sandy laughed. "I just put it on cruise and let it go."

I was feeling reflective and wanted to talk about how Sandy remembered so much and I remembered so little. Our story was so full of layers, and Sandy had always been able to drill through and descend on thin ropes of memory. I dangled above and observed from a sort of cinematic perspective. Often, I only saw what was right in front of me, especially if the stories were difficult.

"Do you think Daddy's suicide and Mama's drinking traumatized you?" I asked, as we rolled through Charlotte.

"At the funeral after his suicide one of our cousins told me, 'That's not your Daddy,'" Sandy said. "It's the first I knew he wasn't. I was more angry than traumatized. I went straight to Mama and that's when she told me my real name was Alverson. From then on I was verbal about our family issues and you kept it all in."

She was right, I did keep it in, especially when I was younger. I went to great lengths to keep from telling others about the troubles at home. The only place I was comfortable with the trouble was around the dining room table on Sundays when we would tell the old stories and laugh.

Outside Wadesboro, North Carolina, by serendipity, we stopped at a light next to a silver historic marker for no one other than Hugh Hammond Bennett, the father of soil conservation and the head of the Service while the work was done in Spartanburg in the 1930s. I asked Sandy to pull over and let me commune for a moment with his unexpected ghost. Bennett had been born in a plantation home nearby in 1881, so as a boy, he'd played, worked, and roamed his father's Piedmont cotton farm. These experiences had let him witness soil erosion while growing up. The old Piedmont farm along Highway 74 had been repurposed. Bennett's "war" against gullies was abandoned decades earlier, and the occupying army was now fast food, lube shops, and little subdivisions.

The two dozen gray granite head stones of the Bennett family cemetery filled a rise south of the highway, but I'd read Bennett isn't buried there. When he died in 1960, he was interred in Arlington National Cemetery, a fitting resting place for a head of one of FDR's army of New Deal agencies.

I gazed east as Sandy waited patiently. I was happy on that high Piedmont hill, connecting geologic dots and not talking about family. I was close to what for me was the mysterious seam between the Piedmont and coastal plain, a significant geographical transition unnoticed by the passing traffic. I stood and pondered the regional differences before we would leave the Piedmont behind. The southern seaboard states are divided into mountains, Piedmont, and coastal plain, like a slice of pie cut into three pieces. As I looked east, I imagined behind me the great rise of the old mountains pushed up like crust and then worn down by eons of erosion, and out in front of me the vanished undulating waves, the ancient seas rising and falling. The sandy soil of the old dunes ahead of us was all that was left of the retreating sea. Harrington had done his magic way back in geology class.

In a few minutes we passed through Rockingham, and I left geology behind and squabbled teasingly with Sandy about a memory. "On one trip back to Southern Pines, Mama's Corvair broke down on this hill, right next to that vanished restaurant called the Orange Bowl," I remembered.

"Mama didn't have a Corvair," Sandy said.

"Well, somebody had a Corvair and it broke down right here on this road."

"Maybe it was one of Mama's brothers?"

"I don't know whose Corvair it was, but we had to get it fixed before we could go on to Southern Pines."

"It's amazing to me you can remember all that, but you can't remember who was driving."

Thirty minutes later we stood in Pinebluff, gazing into a vacant lot where grandfather Lon Brown had tried to burn down his house, with me in it, for insurance money. "That was late 1954 or maybe early '55," Sandy explained. "You weren't a year old. You had been asleep in the crib. I was in the living room playing with my paper dolls when the call went out to clear the house."

"Where was Mama?"

"She must have been at work."

"'Fire, fire!' Granddaddy yelled. Smoke rose from within. Granddaddy had piled oily rags in a corner and set them ablaze."

"Where was Grandmama?"

"She had to be there, maybe in the kitchen fixing lunch. Maybe it was one of our aunts who hustled everybody out."

I looked into the vacant lot. Dark storm clouds pushed down on top of the tall curtain of Longleaf pines and spindly hardwoods. The thick vegetation made it difficult even to imagine the vanished two-story white frame house where my grandparents had lived nearly seventy years earlier.

Sandy wanted to make the remembering easier for me, and so she pulled out an envelope with a half dozen printed pictures she'd collected of the house and family. I flipped through and I saw one of me, a frowning infant in a stroller, our dachshund Paula at my feet. A headless aunt looks on. One girl cousin has turned her back on me. Was my frown an indication of trauma, or just typical momentary infant angst?

"Do you think this photo was before or after the fire?" I asked.

"That picture was taken Easter Sunday," Sandy said. "I remember I had paper dolls. They were important to me because I just got them. I could have gotten them for Christmas."

Another particularly clear photo showed Lon and Hulda on the broad porch of the vanished house with an empty rocking chair behind them; another showed Lon and Hulda again, closer to the camera, with their house blurred behind them. I held that one out at arm's length against the pines.

"How did they get a house like that?" I asked. "What sort of deal did he make with the devil?"

"I don't know," Sandy said. "But I know one thing. He would have collected on that insurance money."

"Was it you who remembered me inside?"

"I turned and went right back inside to get my paper dolls. Somebody brought you out though," Sandy said, smiling. "You're here telling this story, aren't you?"

"When do you think you began to care as much for me as you did your paper dolls?" I asked.

"It took a long time," Sandy said.

"The mayor of the town lived across the street," Sandy continued, pointing to a nice house down from the vanished one of our grandparents. "The mayor knew Lon Brown was a painter and asked him for a bid to paint his house. The mayor decided to go with someone else, so Lon Brown snuck over and put salt in his competitor's paint so it would blister and peel off. Then he told the mayor, maybe he should have taken his bid. Lon Brown ended up repainting the house for the mayor."

I have told friends that our grandfather was a painter; I enjoyed how some assumed I meant he created portraits or landscapes instead of painting exteriors and interiors. In another story Lon Brown had some paint and his brother Grover had a cow. Lon Brown wanted the cow and wanted to trade with his brother for the cow. His brother Grover didn't tell him the cow was sick, and after they made the trade the cow died, Grover used the paint and found out Lon Brown had watered it down.

Some people don't tell dark stories about their families, and Sandy had trouble digging some things up. Some stories, like the near miss in the burning house, are told over and over. After Pinebluff we drove toward Southern Pines, where we were going to meet a cousin for a tour of the area of the county where the Browns, our ancestors, had settled, and Lon Brown had grown up. As we drove Sandy recounted what she knew of the Browns, giving me some background.

The oldest story Sandy had gathered about the Browns was of our third great-grandfather, "a Murray," and she explained how he had serious identity issues. "He was born illegitimate one county over. He never settled on a name. He appeared throughout the middle and late nineteenth century as 'Edmond/Ed/Edward/Coley/Murray.' Coley was his mother's name and Murray was his illegitimate father's name. In spite of these mixed feelings, he did well for himself," Sandy explained as we drove east of Pinebluff toward an area named after our family called Brown's Crossroads.

"Then Edmond/Ed/Edward/Coley/Murray repeated and replicated the complexities of his own origins and had two acknowledged families—seven Murray children from his legitimate marriage to Catherine Ledbetter and two illegitimate children by our third great-grandmother Beedie Ann Carpenter, who was a tenant on his farm. Upon Coley-Murray's death, about 1886, he left a child's share of his property to his illegitimate son John Carpenter, the brother of our then deceased two-time great-grandmother Nellie Anne Carpenter. This instigated a feud and legal battle with our legitimate Murray ancestors that carried over three generations and ended up with a murder in Stanly County in 1917."

To twist things even more, "Nellie Anne Carpenter, the daughter of Beedie Ann Carpenter, had an illegitimate daughter with Caleb Jones Simpson, a local store owner. That child was our great-grandmother Nezzie 'Betty' Elizabeth Carpenter, who then married Mitchell Calvin Brown. In March of 1917, John R. Murray (also known as Coley) and his young son ran into Murray's great-nephews, two of Nezzie and Mitchell Calvin's sons, teenaged Paul and Sam Brown, the older brothers of our grandfather Lon Brown, at Rocky River Springs. A heated argument began, and Lon Brown's older brother Paul shot Murray while his son watched. Great-uncle Paul was convicted of manslaughter and served ten years; Sam did four months on the chain gang. Court papers make it clear that our great-grandmother 'Betty' Carpenter Brown considered her family legitimate heirs to Murray land, and so I maybe can assume this added to the intractable differences between the descendants. Soon after the murder, Mitchell Calvin's family sold their holdings and left Stanly County. The family then moved to the border of Hoke and Moore Counties, not far from here."

We met with our cousin, also named Sandy, and her husband. They had lived elsewhere but kept a condo in Southern Pines to spend time where she'd grown up. I'd never met this cousin and her husband before, and I really enjoyed them. We drove into the country until we reached a four-way blinking stop light, a perfect intersection of two asphalt roads that were once rural. The land was flat in every direction and pine trees filled every empty space. There was an abandoned Mexican restaurant on one corner and there was a colorful convenience store on another, advertising chicken gizzards on the marquee.

"Brown's Crossroads," I said. "The ancient epicenter of this side of our family." Brown's Crossroads was one of my homelands. "Some of your people come from there," Mama had told Sandy.

As her husband pulled over into the parking lot of the abandoned Mexican restaurant, our cousin explained, "We used to call it Buchen Farm, after the old man who owned it before granddaddy."

"So, great-grandpa Brown owned all this?" Sandy asked.

"The house was there where that telephone pole is. He owned hundreds and hundreds of acres," the cousin said. "I heard that, but I don't know that for sure."

I stepped out of the car and crossed the road into the site of the yard where three generations of our ancestors had worked and played. The lot was cleared, grown up in a summer's worth of dog fennel and pokeweed. That corner of the crossroad was still rural. This was near the site of a photo of our grandmother Hulda and eight Browns standing in the field in 1948. Our Mama is peering over her grandfather's shoulder. At first glance it's a perfect agrarian pastoral scene. There are several smiles, but mostly there are grimaces. Grandma anchors the center. She is large-breasted and fills out her simple dress entirely. Ripening tobacco frames the off-kilter shot. The family looks like they're guarding something, maybe the hard past?

As we headed back toward Southern Pines, Sandy continued her deep dive into the Lon Brown saga. "Lon Brown's father Mitchell Calvin and some of his brothers farmed at Brown's Crossroads. Lon Brown had a son by his first wife in Montgomery County, but about that time Lon Brown left the area and ended up in Spartanburg to work in the mill. There he met Hulda Bradley, who would become our grandmother, and married her."

Sandy showed our cousin the pictures she'd showed me from Pinebluff. There was Lon Brown looking back at the camera. I asked our cousin, in her late seventies and old enough to have memories of Lon Brown, what she remembered about our grandfather. She became very reflective: "When stories are passed around, they are subtracted from or added to according to what somebody telling it has perceived," the cousin said. She continued. "I always heard Lon went out for a carton of milk for the family and never came back home, that he met another woman, and had another family, and then later he went back to your grandmother."

I really wanted more than what she was giving us. She sensed it and added, "He was always in and out of our lives. He was outgoing, gregarious, more outgoing than my father and the other brothers. I imagined he had a sense of adventure because he left. Everybody else stuck around here. In my mind Lon was a ladies' man. He was very good looking, and I can see how some of these things could happen. I also knew he was an alcoholic. Mama didn't want Daddy to be around him. Once Lon and his brother Grover came by and

Mama said to my father, 'Barney, you go with them and you will not have a family to come back to.' We didn't do a lot with those other Browns."

"Isn't Lon Brown buried up here?" I asked. Sandy and our cousin answered in the affirmative, and we drove to the cemetery where many of the Browns have gained their eternal rest. We pulled up a gravel drive among the graves and Sandy, our cousin, and our cousin's husband sat in the car while I searched. There was a big standing stone for our great-grandfather Brown and great-grandmother Brown, and there were a dozen other Browns resting in two parallel rows.

"I can't find him," I said, returning to the car, and Sandy and our cousin stepped out. We crossed the gravel road and discovered Lon's flat stone resting at the head of his brother Grover, the drinker, the one Lon had cheated in the paint deal. Lon Brown's stone had sunk into the ground and one corner stuck up and it been gnawed down by some beast or lawnmower, a fitting testimony to a man who was always restlessly working some angle.

Slump

World War II wounded my father in ways I'd tried to understand. He was a combat engineer, a bridge builder, he fought in North Africa and Sicily, and landed in the second wave at Omaha Beach, then fought his way on across Europe. Daddy drank a quart of whiskey a day once he was out of the Army. I guess you would say he was a functional alcoholic. He came back broken but carried on anyway as if he wasn't—he married, performed as stepfather to Sandy, fathered me, ran a service station in Southern Pines, and later, an upholstery shop in Aberdeen.

About 1948, Mama moved from Florida to Brown's Crossroads and worked in nearby Aberdeen in a restaurant. "That's where Mama and Daddy met," Sandy remembered. "They went out to the honky-tonks and probably drank together. Moore County was dry, and so they might have gone to the VFW club." Sandy said Daddy took to carrying her around. "They married back in Spartanburg, in Saxon in '49 at the Methodist parsonage. Mama's sister Lottie and her husband Norman were the witnesses."

The quart of whiskey Daddy drank should have been a sign, but Mama seemed content with men who drank too much, like Lon Brown and some of her brothers. After Mama and Daddy married he curtailed his drinking, and about 1949 he took a job as a lineman in Kensington, Maryland. He moved Mama and Sandy into an apartment up there, but soon depression set in. Daddy's brother Sidney drove up and hauled them all back to the family farm in Greene County, North Carolina, where they lived for a few months as he recovered. The Lanes were tobacco farmers, working the same ground for at least five previous generations. Most remained to farm either the family land or other farms they acquired or rented. Daddy's family was huge, just like Mama's—nine brothers and sisters, all grown

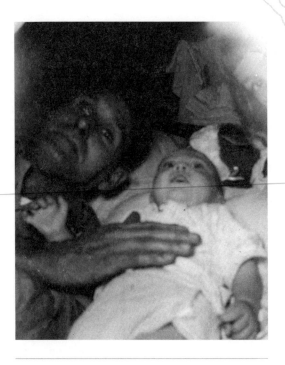

John Lane, Johnny Lane, and Sandra Alverson
Blurred in Corner, Southern Pines, N.C.
(Mary Ellen Brown Lane, 1955)

up on the Lane family farm near Wilson, North Carolina, a hundred miles east of Southern Pines and Pinebluff, more flat coastal plain sandy loam. "Mama finally said she put her foot down and said they couldn't stay there and live off the Lanes forever."

Once Mama, Daddy, and Sandy left the Lane farm and went back to Southern Pines, life improved slowly. They lived in a trailer behind Daddy's brother Julian's service station. They used the bathroom there. Daddy fished in a small boat wearing what looked like an Army dress cap. He sold cars for another brother, Sidney. They were all farm boys from eastern North Carolina back from the war. Then Daddy, Mama, and Sandy moved into a block house behind the station that Sandy loved. Sandy got her first dog there, and somehow Daddy landed a lease on the Gulf station right across the street from Julian's Shell station on Highway One.

Things went well for a while. Daddy somehow kept the ticking time bomb of his mental illness buried in the Southern Pines sand. He ran the Gulf station on Highway One, the main north-south route to Florida. He cared for his young family—his wife, stepdaughter Sandy, his young son (once I came along), and he bought his own two-story frame house downtown on Ashe Street. He had two cars and there was a piano in the parlor. He put in a garden every spring for almost a decade. Mama was a hostess at the Howard Johnson's. Life looked up. I was born in October of 1954, the month of the biggest North Carolina storm for decades, Hurricane Hazel, which pushed all the way inland to Southern Pines. Mama said that she shared a hospital room with Babe Zaharias, the most famous female golfer of her time, living then in Pinehurst. She said Babe held me in her arms and rocked me. It was my birth myth, that I was born next to greatness, a short distance away across the room.

Mama had her problems with drinking too. Once when Mama and Daddy lived in the block house behind his brother's station, Mama brought a man home in the middle of the day. Daddy's brother saw them, and Daddy put Mama and Sandy on the train to Spartanburg. Mama claimed the man was an old friend and they were just drinking coffee. Daddy later took her back in. Mama hid her bottles under the stairway on Ashe Street. Sandy saw Mama's hiding place and told Daddy. He came home and found the bottle. "He sat at the kitchen table, poured them both a shot, and told Mama not to hide drinking. It was the only time I ever saw Daddy drink," Sandy said.

Besides the drinking, Daddy and Mama began to have money problems. In the late 1950s, the Highway One bypass opened around Southern Pines and Daddy's Gulf station closed. They rented the top floor of the Ashe Street house to a stock car racer, his wife, and their toddler. For months before he killed himself, Daddy wanted out. He slashed his wrists at the upholstery shop in Aberdeen. "I was with Mama the day he did it, but I didn't really understand." There were other times too. Mama stopped working her shifts at the Howard Johnson and tried to hide the keys to the car.

Daddy didn't hold together very long at a time. Those years, there were at least two stints in the VA hospital in Fayetteville after the suicide attempts. The hospital did little good. Mama said the hospital may have made things worse. When he came home, Daddy sat and watched TV, deep in the darkness that eventually enveloped him. The only time Sandy saw Daddy come out of it was once when a 1940s song came on the radio. "He stood up and did the jitterbug," she said.

In Southern Pines we had a dog named Paula, a black dachshund, and when I was toddler, she went into heat and Mama and Daddy kept her inside. A shoal of hormone-mad male dogs from the neighborhood surged back and forth outside. One day I leaned against the door and Paula slipped out and I followed, and I fell among the dogs. I was bitten on the lip and had to go through the rabies series—twenty-one shots in the belly.

I still have a scar on my upper lip, so I remember the dogs.

There was always some contradiction in the family about this story, and it usually surfaced around the dining room table on Sunday at the midday meal we call "dinner." Sunday dinner was a tradition that stretched back as far as I can remember and only ceased in 1997 when Mama's health started to fail. Mama remembered the story the way I told it—but one Sunday a decade or so before Mama died, Sandy said she remembered it another way.

"You and I were on the porch and I was looking after you. Paula was with us and there were three or four male dogs below and you fell down into them. Daddy was outside with us. He waded in and kicked the dogs off."

The way Mama and I remembered the story placed Mama in the best light. She was a good mother and the baby was safe inside. Somebody just forgot to latch the door. Sandy's version highlights the complexity of our family's situation at that time. It was us, the two kids, caught outside in a perilous world crazy as mad dogs massed below us. Daddy was the hero.

On the November night Daddy killed himself, he stopped at Sandy's downstairs bedroom door and asked, "Sandy, are you awake?" Then said it one more time. He walked out to the car and attached the vacuum hose to the green station wagon's exhaust and closed himself up within. Sandy was mad at him that night and she laid there and didn't answer. She was twelve years old, angry about something Daddy told her she couldn't do, the routine petulance of teenage years coming on in any normal life, though little was normal in that house. Sandy knows that had she climbed out of bed she would only have postponed the inevitable. The bomb had dropped long before. Blame it on the war years and the combat he saw—World War II's version of PTSD. He'd been depressed his whole life. His cousin Jenny Wooten described him to me as a "melancholy boy."

A week before Daddy killed himself Mama wrote to our grandmother in St. Augustine, where Hulda and Lon Brown had moved again. She asked Lon to sell a lot to help them out, explaining how desperate the situation had become. "He has one good day and then a real bad one," Mama wrote. "He sleeps about two hours a night and I have to keep my eyes on him all the time. As for myself I'm real proud I haven't drank a drop since he came home, and I don't want any. I can't understand because I got more on me now than I ever had in my life . . . I don't think he'll last much more than a week here at home not unless he gets better."

Mama found him soon after she woke up and came downstairs. She'd slept upstairs that night because it had all become too much.

Maybe it wasn't exactly an explosion we experienced that night. Maybe it was more geological. Slump is known as a form of mass wasting. A slope that looks stable can collapse in an instant—landslides, rock falls. Debris slide. Mud flow. Earth flow. What we think is solid is often in motion if the conditions are right. It happens over time and then the collapse is sudden. A slow process of gravitational pull, slope angle, and all types of weathering lead to catastrophe. Our exposed lives slid that night, a lifetime's erosion in an evening, and it would take a decade or more to get them back together.

Years later a Southern Pines cousin told me she went to yard sales to look for "old dress patterns," and one Saturday found a box packed tight and going back to the 1960s. She knew because the box was padded with period newspapers. As she looked through the patterns and took them out of the box, she finally reached the bottom padded with a newspaper from a day in November of 1959. A name she knew caught her eye. "Staring up at me was the front-page story reporting your father's suicide."

When I was young, Sandy was my only possible protector against the building chaos of the family. Mama was drinking bad after Daddy died. Sandy took care of me, but she was often irritated by her little brother's showing up when she didn't expect me or want me around. I'd sneak out of the house and follow her a half mile to the nearby stables where she rode and cared for the horses she loved. The route went through a deep gully and up and over a sand ridge. When Sandy was out the door, I'd follow her, sneaking just far enough behind to stay hidden. I followed over and over. Sandy finally got me to stop by telling me, "A huge wall of water's gonna come down that gully and wash you away." I was five years old. I've been running from that gully-washer ever since. For years I had a dream in which I was out in front of the wave, never looking back.

When I try to understand our family's collapse and Daddy's early death at forty-four, I think through my own early attempts to write. I didn't write much about feelings early on. I wrote instead in images and descriptive prose. I never stated anything straight up. I liked writing about places, landscapes, and animals. When I thought deeply about something it was the earth and its deep history. I could get emotional about road cuts and soil profiles and gullies. Daddy's death left a hole in me that was never filled.

One day in the bookshop in downtown Spartanburg a very elegantly dressed gray-haired gentleman wandered over. I recognized him as a former French professor at a local college. He carried a nonfiction book he planned to buy called *D-Day Girls*. "You must like to read about D-Day," I said. "My father was there, Omaha Beach. I stood on the beach two summers ago," thinking I had the upper hand.

"How did it feel?" he asked, surprising me a little.

"The heavy seas looked just like they must have the morning he landed," I said. "I felt like I was there with him. I felt as close to Daddy as I ever have. I didn't really know him."

Then the man said, "I was there too, that June morning in 1944. I was three."

He'd lived in Caen, seven miles back from the landing beaches, and because of the bombing he'd slept fitfully the night before. His parents had moved him from his bedroom into theirs in the three-story apartment building downtown. That morning a bomb exploded and destroyed all but the room they were, all three, sleeping in.

"Daddy took me in his arms and opened the door and stepped through. We fell two floors. There was so much dust in the air he couldn't see the stairway was blown away. I suffered a cut on my head, but besides that, we were all fine."

"That was ten years before I was born," I said. "My father committed suicide when I was five. What do you remember from when you were three?"

"Images," he said. "Fragments. When the house blows up it makes an impression upon you."

Mary Ellen Brown Lane and Johnny Lane, Florida Avenue,
Spartanburg, S.C. (Sandy Alverson Camby, 1963)

Downtown Gullies

In June of 1960, after school let out for Sandy in Southern Pines, Mama packed up the light green station wagon Daddy had killed himself in and we moved to Spartanburg. It must have felt like retreating to a cave of the familiar for Mama. She must have felt like a hunted animal after all the years Daddy was in and out of hospitals and then his series of suicide attempts. Her own craving for alcohol must have made it worse. Within a year after arriving in Spartanburg, Mama lost the house in Southern Pines and most of the furniture. "She never talked about that much," Sandy said. "A realtor rented it out after we left, but she told me later she couldn't pay the taxes on it and the county sold the house. I can remember she felt foolish for not getting any money for the house at all."

Before Mama retreated to Spartanburg, she'd been drinking bad in Southern Pines. She was only thirty-four, but she'd already tried and failed AA. Lon Brown didn't help. He drank with her in those months after Daddy died. Maybe Mama and Lon Brown got along so well after he reappeared because they could share a bottle.

Sandy headed west toward downtown. "Do you remember we used to get barbeque at Cherry Hill?" she asked.

"I'm not sure," I answered, not ready yet to drop back into the past. "It's the type of detail I think I remember, but it could be that I'd heard it mentioned so many times in the family stories."

In Spartanburg, direction was allegory, and in many ways, direction had also always been destiny. Taking Morgan Square as the magic center of Spartanburg's urban compass, west was endless nuevo estates, the gateway to over-hyped Greenville, thirty miles away; north was Smurf houses and metastasizing suburban sprawl, the old orchards filled with patio-home developments one at a time toward the hazy Blue Ridge; south was wild and rural, broom sedge fields, a few cattle farms, and much of what was left, hunting land; and east was big trees, the first country club, older and settled neighborhoods, including what Mama always called "Pill Hill." But if you go out east you pass where Sandy and Don live. It's where they raised their two children, my nephew Sean and my niece Lyn. Sandy and Don moved there and not somewhere else so Don could be close to Broome High School, where he was an assistant principal for twelve years. They live about as far east as you can and still say you are in Spartanburg. A mile further they'd have to claim the town of Cowpens as a mailing address. I can't imagine Sandy and Don living anywhere else.

Further east, just over the Pacolet River, you get rural again, but east rural had its own tone, at least along East Main Street after it turned into Highway 29, the old highway to Charlotte before I-85; out there it was tumbled-down textile mills along the river, more like the villages the Bradleys would recognize.

Once back in Spartanburg, Mama crowded her shell-shocked family into her half-sister's house downtown on the corner of Woodward Avenue and Nash Street. Sandy pulled up at the empty lot where our aunt's house had once stood. Grandmama lived only two blocks away on Hall Street, and after all, Mama had only been away about a decade.

I looked north and considered the erosion of forgetting, an active process like the accumulation of remembering. I looked all around trying to get oriented. When we arrived in Spartanburg, we took up residence at our aunt's house right across the street from a gully. That first summer in town I would have looked out at the gulch between the aunt's house and the next ridge and maybe wondered where I had landed. But maybe I wouldn't have noticed the gully at all.

By June of '60 I was almost six years old. I should have been old enough to recall a few episodes. Sometimes I think I ought to be able to lay it all out and put all that happened back then in line the way Sandy could with the dates on old photos, but it was never that simple with memory.

What had I been told? What did I make up? What was forgotten that might be key to sorting sense out of my past?

Maybe my forgetting meant that I had a certain charm—missing the hurricane by a week or so when I was born, escaping the house fire my grandfather had set, surviving the fall into the pack of dogs. Gathering a few good stories would be the shovel to dig out from under a slump.

Sandy said, "The house had a big porch and a water oak next door."

"I remember the neighbors had a chain over a limb to work on cars."

"The house was only a few blocks from the jewelry counter where Mama in 1945 had met my Daddy and where she'd walked with a stroller only a year later and run into W. C. Alverson again after he'd left her."

Sandy told these sad stories with no emotion. "Mama told me she followed Daddy down to Morgan Hotel to shack up."

"Where did we all sleep at our aunt's?"

"We probably pushed somebody out and slept on pallets," Sandy said as we sat and stared at the empty lot and the lonely oak. "The house had one floor and six rooms, with a big hall down the middle and bedrooms and a living room off to each side, the boys in one room girls in another, and a kitchen on the back."

Sandy said we stayed at our aunt's for about two months. I have one clear memory of that house. There was a neighborhood boy killed in an auto accident, and his parents laid him out in an open casket in the front room of the house on the corner. I asked Sandy if she remembered. "I think he was a friend of the family and we all went to view the body."

"That was likely a few years later," Sandy said. "When we visited Woodward Avenue. Our aunt lived there through most of the '6os."

We drove down the street. There were two or three remaining houses with wide porches, painted wood frames, and in the eaves, a few surviving Victorian gingerbread flourishes. These houses were once middle-class merchant bungalows, already thirty years past their prime and fading by 1960 when we arrived.

The Spartanburg Mama and Sandy had left in the late 1940s had been a typical small southern town, organized around a strong central urban core and circled by thriving textile villages and still-working agricultural lands, many of the hills covered in peach orchards.

After our return I became familiar with walking the busy streets of that small, thriving southern city with its big department stores and corner neighborhood stores. That was before strip malls, before QuikTrip, even Krispy Kreme. The major streets back then were two lanes at best, and it would be a decade before streets were widened to four-lane thoroughfares for moving traffic from booming east and west sides.

By 1960 new forces were pulling at our fragile world. The strict class and color lines would soon ease a little, and the collapse of the urban Spartanburg was already under way. During the decades of the 1960s and 1970s, the outer brick ranch house suburbs developed to the city's East. By 1960 the imposing 1920s two-story downtown high school, a few blocks away from our aunt's house, had moved to the eastside suburbs.

When we left my aunt's old street, Sandy cut up past where our grandmother Hulda Brown died. I had few memories of grandparents. When it came to family, I was like a coastal plain pine with its roots stretching out in a shallow mat. A good wind could tilt me over. My paternal grandfather Lane died at ninety-two years old in 1963. Sandy said we visited him a few times at the eastern North Carolina farm before he died. Though I was nine years old the memories were thin, only a few stranded stories my North Carolina aunts told me— how stern he was with his five sons, and how that was probably what drove Daddy to Southern Pines, how, born less than a decade after the Civil War, he never owned a tractor but plowed with a mule his whole life, how in old age he went to Atlantic Beach and sat all day at the Pavilion so he could "watch the pretty girls go by."

My maternal grandfather, Lon Brown? He died in 1966 but he was the object of so many of the family's most memorable tales. Lon Brown was deeply complex, and nothing that comes of telling these stories has settled that complexity. He was like those buried organic deposits Terry had discovered in the gullies.

Lon Brown was a character. He was both villain and hero. The numerous photos of Lon Brown as a young man showed him lean and angular in glasses with swept-back hair. He was listed on his draft registration papers as ruddy, with a scar behind his right ear of adequate size to note. Ruddy and scarred. No wonder he would come to loom so big in my mind. The family stories, of which there were many, made him out to be a flimflam man, philanderer, con man, gyp artist, check and deed forger, horse trader, swindler, thief. He was like literature itself, resisting paraphrase.

If not paraphrase, what conclusions could I draw from Lon Brown's remembered stories? In hindsight the easiest thing in the world would be to judge Lon Brown too harshly. Maybe my judgment was a form of Romanticism, but I imagined Lonnie as a sort of character in a southern Gothic short story, someone a good writer might have revised out as too common a freak—bigamist, thief, drunk. Maybe Lon's early transgressions could be understood as signs of hard times that I had not experienced.

Maybe the positive guiding spirit of Lon Brown was alive in me—that "adventurer" my Brown cousin had called him. But maybe not. Maybe I had slipped past his shadow and made my own way in the world. I stole no hubcaps and forged only report cards, not deeds or felony checks. The paint I apply was not watered down.

And my grandmothers? My paternal grandmother Lane died when Daddy was overseas in World War II, twelve years before I was born, though her large, oval, early twentieth-century portrait hangs in our bedroom. She was dressed in a black dress with a high collar. It was like having Emily Dickinson staring at me every morning as I brushed my teeth. I kept her there on the wall watching me, because every summer as a child I visited an aunt's house in eastern North Carolina, and the portrait hung in the bedroom where I stayed. Years later, when the aunt died, the nieces and nephews gathered in the family home for a dispersion lottery. I drew a high number. Rather than select the family china or the Civil War–era blanket chest, I took home the portrait. The vestige of grandmother Lane, long dead, reminded me that even if memory doesn't survive, faces do.

The pictures I had of my maternal grandmother Hulda Brown were smaller—snapshots—and I had kept them mostly packed away. What feelings I did have were a sort of thin silt that rolled in any time Sandy pulled out the photos or started telling stories about Hulda. My grandmother was not a living entity—at least not for me. I didn't remember finding comfort in her broad presence prowling in a house dress. I had no memory of childhood sanctuary discovered in her ample bosom. "She was pretty somber most of the time," Sandy said when I asked what she remembered. "She was not somebody you would go and love on."

According to accounts passed down, everybody liked something Granny cooked. Her biscuits were legend. I'd often wondered if Mama's cooking skills came directly from her mother. The twins used to play practical jokes on her all the time—once one loaded a pistol with blanks and fired it at the other while our grandmother watched. About Hulda's early death at fifty-four, Sandy explained: "She had a lot of health problems. Her death was sudden, a stroke."

"That's where she lived," Sandy said, pointing to a duplex apartment on Hall Street. "One aunt told me when she died the family was thrown into a turmoil. Where would they have the home visitation? Another aunt even used the event as a chance to be petty. She went into Granny's apartment, found a newspaper clipping of when Mama was caught for drunk driving, and put it on the mantel for everyone to see."

Shouldn't I have remembered something about her death? I was seven. Sandy said I would have seen her regularly that year we were back in Spartanburg. Her death in 1961 was not my ground zero. The death of Daddy was less than two years earlier. No wonder all that feeling about my grandmother was buried for years.

We drove further east. The first place of our own back in Spartanburg was a duplex on Hollywood Street. I turned six on Hollywood but I didn't start school until that next September. I went to first grade at Southside Elementary and then we moved in March. They held me back that year. What happened? My report card shows I had too many absences. I guess that means Mama was already drinking heavily.

We drove past the duplex. "That's where one of the twins and J. C. got drunk and the police chased them, and they fell into a train cut behind the house," Sandy remembered.

"Mama always called it a gully when she told the story," I added. "It had that feeling, a slash into level land."

The trains still run through the man-made gully behind it.

We drove back into the city to East Park Avenue, where we'd lived a short time in a small rental house. The house had been torn down many years before. "It was an old house. The windows leaked," Sandy conjured, looking up into the bare lot.

I remembered nothing of our social life there. All I remembered was landscape. "Down the street was a creek but it had been put in a culvert. Further on it ran free over broken asphalt and cement slabs. When the rains fell in the creek boiled with the runoff from the city streets."

"The sidewalk was pushed up by roots."

"Across the street was a house with no underpinning. Exposed pipes. A scary place."

"A large family had lived there. I played with their kids. Under the house was a place to explore. Once I was under their house and I saw something white in the darkness. I watched the shape fade away and I thought it was the form of a cat. That was my first ghost."

Next we drove out to the Howard Johnson's where Mama worked her first job after we returned to Spartanburg. Somehow it still stands out on the interstate after almost sixty years, a spirit from my childhood, a resistant ridge of family memory in a gully of passing time. We drove out there and Sandy and I talked after parking out front. The restaurant was boarded up, but it still had the orange California tile roof line that made it seem so exotic in a mill town in the 1960s. The pool Sandy said we swam in had been filled.

We looked into the wreck of a lobby where Mama had handed out menus to travelers southbound on the newly opened I-85.

In back we saw troupes of interstate itinerants living in what used to be the motor lodge. I looked around the corner and then pulled back. I was looking into Cormac McCarthy's future apocalypse, *The Road*. Broken, cast-off families milled about. The doors to the rooms were wide open, funneling in the breeze, in the absence of air conditioning. Several men, like sentinels, eyed me suspiciously—as if I might be the bearer of an expected eviction notice or a contractor looking the real estate over for redevelopment. Little did they know the aging man in the new pickup was eyeing them too, looking for kinship, as if they might offer some clue to his own personal landscape if things in the 1960s had gone a different way.

Then we drove back into the city, ping-ponging among our past residences. We drove out South Church Street to the mill village of Arkwright. The house was on Woodlawn Street, just "off village," and was still occupied. "There's a junk car in the side yard and a kitchen chair out front," I said as we approached.

The old house was painted yellow. "Look at those white awnings with a cursive S still shading the windows, just like in a snapshot I have from that year," Sandy said.

When we pulled up an old man wandered down the street. He had a big gray beard, and a beat-up Tarheel cap, an oversized camo tee shirt, and sweatpants. I got out of the car and asked if anybody lived there. "Me," he answered.

The old man was talkative. He said he was originally from Pauline, and I asked if I could take a picture of the house with him in it, so he shuffled into the dirt yard and dropped his arms to his side, looked through me, much in the way I was looking through him into the past. The house seemed tiny now. What I remembered was not the details but the poverty, the wooden mill houses, and the old convertible Mama had.

"Mama loved convertibles," Sandy said.

"I pulled our passed-out mother off the floor heat grate," I said, remembering. "The hot metal had burned her arm. Later, when she wore short sleeves, we could always see the scar, a grid that looked like a tic-tac-toe board."

"Mama planned my fourteenth birthday party here. 'We're new in town. Let's have a party,' Mama said. I invited my new school friends, and Mama bought hotdogs and drinks. But it was the first of the month, and the minute the checks came, Mama got drunk. I had to call everyone and cancel," Sandy explained. "If she was drunk after that, I'd just lock her in her bedroom and have the party anyway."

There was once a huge fig tree in the backyard, big enough to crawl into. The leaves were the size of the double hands of a child. The fruit was probably some of the first I'd ever harvested myself. Sweet and soft. Birds, black birds, grackles, ate most of the fruit that spring.

"Do you still have a floor furnace?" I asked the old man, thinking about Mama's fall and the scar on her arm.

"It's gone. But a big ceiling fan keeps it cool."

"Is that your garden? Is there still a fig tree back there?"

"I'm trying to keep the corn alive," he answered. "Been dry. No fig. All that's back there is that old pecan."

We pull up out front on Pierpont Avenue Extension, our next house, where a man and a woman watched me get out and snap a picture. I waved and I said, "We used to live here."

"That's where you stayed? Mexicans are fixing it up now," the man said.

"Yes, and that was where Mrs. Trakas lived," I said, speaking of my friend Deno's grandmother.

"Oh, we knew Miss Virginia, and her sister Miss Bessie lived over there," the woman said, pointing next door. "They passed a long time ago."

"Is that big flat rock still down in the creek?"

"Yeah, it's still there. That's a pretty little creek."

"Any way to get down there?"

"You could go in from the other way," she said, gesturing toward the spindly trees and weeds. "There's a path. They do drugs down there. You might get jumped."

"Ok, maybe we won't go." We both laughed.

"I bet there's still little fish down there though."

"Are the terraces still in the back?"

"We cleared them off and tried to grow a garden."

"And you know, there used to be a trailer park over there."

"Oh yeah, I remember that trailer park. Gone now but I lived there once. Long time ago."

We drove back to the north side of town, to Florida Avenue. The house there was gone. "Look," Sandy said. "Mintz scrap bought it and tore it down."

A huge heap of scrap metal loomed behind a chain link fence. We rented that Florida Avenue house for two years, the longest we stayed anywhere in the first years back. Though we were there the longest, it's where the idea of home fell apart. It was the darkest period of Mama's drinking.

In front of our house a path went down to Church Street. The path cut beside some woods, crossed a gully and a creek, then went up another hill, and emptied in the paved parking lot of the 7–11 where I bought Freeze Pops. This gully was a chore, a trash dump, something to pass through quickly, to get to the store and back home. That gully was where we found our little dog.

"Remember we had two dogs? That one somebody shot, and another that disappeared and then turned up months later again," Sandy said. "I think somebody picked it up down at the 7–11."

Dogs and houses blur together. There were six rentals in eight years, 1960–1969—our aunt's house on Woodward, Hollywood Street, Washington Road, Pierpont Avenue Extension, Arkwright, Florida Avenue, Swanee Street—why did we move so much? "Mama couldn't pay the rent," Sandy said.

"She told me, I kept you out of those trailer parks," I remembered.

Childhood back in Spartanburg was unsettled. But everything wasn't a gully. I made my own way. I am surprised I remember so much. I was ten and eleven. I wrote a poem called "The Big Snow" about a storm the first winter, and the teacher copied it on a flip pad and displayed it in the school lobby. I sang in the chorus but had to quit it to play basketball. I tried to play baseball but couldn't catch or throw. My best friend's sister was my first girlfriend. She played basketball better than any of the boys and her brother played guitar and sang "Love Potion Number 9" with me in front of the class at recess. I drank extra milk at lunch, often my only full meal of the day.

There was a program called Scholastic Reader where I could order books and they'd get delivered to class once a month. I preferred sports biographies. I checked a book out of the library over and over about a lobster living deep under the sea.

Mama bought an old set of children's Bible stories illustrated by Albrecht Dürer. I don't remember reading the stories, but I can still close my eyes and see Dürer's dark engraved visions of the flood, the walk out of Egypt, the crucifixion. These must have lined up well with what I experienced at home those years in the mid-1960s, for at times it must have seemed like I was on a journey of trials and calamities. A flood that could cover the known world must have seemed real to me.

We also had a glossy set of supermarket encyclopedias that took up shelf space usually filled by Mama's ceramic knickknacks; each color volume purchased with Top Value stamps. I soon learned I preferred fact to fiction, the globe laid open A to Z, an orderly cosmos to pour out nightly in the den, a river of knowledge, each book a waterfall of reality.

In a year or two I read through the known world, from Aardvarks to Zoos. The story of my life was harder to contain. When my mother wailed in the back bedroom, her cries were less real than Epiphytes, Erosion, Labor Day, Rome, or Wales. I was relieved the stamps didn't run out before the volumes accumulated; Mama completed the set. I met these books head on, open pages crusting my young boy's open mind.

Sandy showed me a picture from that time and said Mama looked "lit" in it. When Mama was drunk she would call anybody, including the president, governor, mayor, and other prominent people if she could find their numbers. That was at the height of Mama's drinking, so nothing was ever certain, especially around the first of the month when the checks arrived. After the first, Mama always left me alone, came home drunk in cabs, and the drivers helped her in.

Florida Avenue was where I started exploring more widely. Maybe the fog from my father's suicide was lifting. Or maybe it was just the freedom given me by my absentee mother. I had a blue Schwinn Stingray with fastback handlebars, silver glow banana saddle, slick rear tire, and three-speed Stik-Shift. Just like Sandy, I was on my own. I'd ride my bike in every direction—over to the hospital, up Dakota Street to the top of the hill, through the trailer park, to the end of the street to a friend's house. Or down to the mud flats next to the creek where a few years later they would build the Dodge dealership.

It was down there I discovered the crumbled edges of an old dam on the creek, what I found out later was the remains of the city's first water reservoir. I'd ride there, hide my bike, and walk along the creek and find pools where I could fish for knotty heads. I still remember how I felt in that deep dark valley—safe, secret, hidden from home.

After Florida Avenue Sandy suggested we eat lunch at Sugar 'n' Spice, an old fast food restaurant that opened soon after we moved back. The old wavy awning out front was bent and flaking orange paint, all that's left from when curb hops worked there. We parked under the awning and headed inside to order. We both knew there were a bunch more stories to tell about us and Mama, about the flash floods we negotiated as a family through the 1960s. Sugar 'n' Spice seemed the right place to terminate our interrogation of the past.

I felt full after our long family tour of the city and the outlying neighborhoods. Settled at a table I looked around. The dining room sheltered a mix of local people—Black, white, rich, poor, young, old. After living in town for sixty years I felt I was one of them, just another regular at the Sugar 'n' Spice.

"We did all right after we landed in Spartanburg," I said. "We survived."

"Barely," Sandy said, smiled, and sipped her tea.

"What better way to celebrate our success than to split a large souvlaki."

"I ate here all the time in high school," she said. "In the early '60s."

"I didn't really start coming until college."

"One time I pulled up in Mama's Oldsmobile and the car hop came over and said, 'Hey, your mama owes me for a pint.'"

Ruins of Enoree Flume with Canoe (John Lane, 2020)

Enoree Flume

Hans Albert Einstein, the first son of the famous physicist Albert Einstein, was a European-trained engineer, and in the late 1930s he moved to Greenville, South Carolina, with his young family to work for a division of the Soil Conservation Service. Hans Albert went on to a distinguished academic career at UC–Berkeley, but in his first posting in Greenville he served as a soldier in SCS director Hugh Hammond Bennett's war on soil erosion. While in Greenville, Hans Albert worked to understand the periodic flush of sediment down the Enoree River, one of many streams dissecting the southern Piedmont. Because he was interested in visible phenomena, it could cleverly be said that Hans Albert's interests were actually parallel to mine. He was interested in the results of gullying in the Piedmont, for there would be no sediment in the river if not for the upstream gullies. Also, like me, he was plunged into the complexities of family, since he had frequent contact with his famous physicist father about a concrete, river-wide research flume built on the Enoree.

With Hans Albert's life and work on my mind, I drove over to the Enoree in late October. I had arranged to meet Dan Richter for a short canoe trip down the river to commune with the flume where Hans Albert had conducted his research. A great deal had changed on the landscape in the eighty years separating me in time from Hans Albert, though there were a few connecting sutures. Albert Einstein's first son had become an American citizen before a judge in Spartanburg in 1943, and in the days when Hans Albert lived in Greenville, he had worked near Greer, fourteen miles closer to Spartanburg. In 1938, when Hans Albert arrived, there was only a winding two-lane highway between the two cities. Now I-85 is six

lanes wide, and that artificial, human-constructed circulatory sys
tem drives our economy. Back then, it was still the farmland itself
that drove life.

Since I-85 was first paved in the late 1950s, it had channeled tons
of chemicals and carcinogens into every stream I crossed. We had
experienced a rainy year. Once the numbers were in, it was the wet-
test year in the Piedmont since 1908. Because of runoff, it would
have been hard on the streams and the life within. As I crossed
each bridge, I tried to get a glimpse of the flow below. Just outside
Spartanburg, the North Tyger River, a sister to the Enoree, had been
impounded in the last century, and the wider, swollen surface of the
resulting lake was easy to see as I crossed. The water's tint in the
early sun was cantaloupe colored, though it had not rained in a few
days. I imagined the red clay washed off ridges upstream, hanging
suspended there until it dropped out, finally settling as sediment on
the bottom where catfish cruised.

Besides the sediment passing down every river, chemicals associated with the exhaust and leakage of internal combustion engines
and interstate transportation were washed off the highway. Those
gasses fell back to earth to form a Latinate litany: carbon dioxide,
carbon monoxide, unburnt hydrocarbons, ammonia, hydrogen sul-
phide, sulphates, ketones, phenols, polycyclic aromatic hydrocarbons, particulate matter, and heavy metals. Those pollutants are a
sort of toxic poll tax we have to pay the river for driving over.

I tried to forget chemistry and the highways that place all those
substances in our rivers. I sped through a thick concentration of fac-
tories and industrial outposts—distribution warehouses, lay-down
lots where building materials are stored, borrow pits—where rolling
Piedmont swales of the natural landscape had been flattened in construction, and at some point in the past activated the transportation of millions of tons of red sediment into the rivers that eternally
drained the sites. Not that those who built didn't know that sediment was toxic too, particularly to aquatic wildlife; but construction
continued in a boom region like the Piedmont, and the poison was
only slowed slightly by government-mandated silt fences. "Runoff"

was a constant poorly monitored pollution in our rivers, another name for Hans Albert's bed load.

The Enoree, Hans Albert's lab site over eighty years ago, was a silty river by any measure. Even on a dry day the color and texture of the flow was chocolate mixed with water. Sometimes it was worse than that, and the eddies and meanders offered up chemical mysteries. I remembered on other visits to the stream that sometimes when the late afternoon light hit the river, I had seen pools of chemical green expanding and contracting on the surface. There was nothing you would call fresh and clean about the Enoree.

But I was a river optimist, a booster, a walking pep rally for moving water, no matter how compromised, how polluted, how silted up by modernity's projects. All rivers were beautiful. I knew that to say that my destination, the Enoree, was beautiful is a complicated assertion. The Enoree's meaning and value had to be filtered through our understanding of millions of years of natural and human history. We must consider its full length, from its head near the Blue Ridge Mountains to its feet dangling into the Broad River, forty miles southeast. But mostly it was easiest to apply scrutiny to the last two hundred years. Working with Terry had shown me how a beautiful Piedmont river like the Enoree could be distorted by two hundred years of heavy human use. That idea highlighted the primary project of the first half of this story about the Piedmont, my coming to terms with how people had altered the landscape.

I realized that in the second half of the story, things got more personal. My people never farmed the gullied fields sloping to the channel of the Enoree or worked the cotton mills below along its course, but they did plenty of damage to the land in adjacent watersheds of the Tyger and Pacolet Rivers. Their farming kept them alive, but it also functioned as an element of erosion. Their mill work functioned in the same way, once removed. They spun cotton fibers grown in southern fields.

Hans Albert worked near the beginning of science's understanding of how impaired our relationship to rivers had become since the Industrial Revolution. As I pulled off the interstate at Pelham Road and made my way to my rendezvous point with Dan, I became more and more interested in dropping a canoe in the Enoree, becoming a passionate observer of human and natural history, and seeing what we could make of the river eighty years after Hans Albert.

The plan we'd made earlier was to meet up at a Vietnamese Catholic church, at what would be our Enoree paddling trip's takeout. It was Sunday after lunch and the last of the mass attendants filtered out and climbed into their cars as I pulled up, leaving the parking lot mostly to us. Richter had texted to say he'd be a little late because of traffic on I-85, so I walked down to scout the riverfront one more time. We'd take out there on a flat outcrop of bedrock alongside the river where the parishioners had set up a fire pit and several red plastic Adirondack chairs. I fired up my iPhone and saw from Google Earth the flume's eighty-year-old cream-colored, concrete comb in the riverbed downstream from a river feature known as Horseshoe Bend. In reality, the flume was just out of sight upstream at the upward end of Gibbs Shoals, a rocky half-mile-long passage.

I looked upstream and could sense the power of approaching the historic feature in a canoe. I was already shaping the story of the day in my mind, even though it hadn't happened yet. All experience to me had the shape of story and sometimes my friends kidded me about that. "To you, the flume is a story element," Terry had said about this outing when we talked earlier. "For those in Greenville or Greer, who knows it exists? What is it? Who would have knowledge or skills even to find out if they discovered it? It looks most like a bridge. Everybody repeats the same old heritage stuff."

I walked back a hundred yards to the parking lot just as Richter's pickup arrived. After our paddle trip he planned to drive thirty miles to Union County to tend to some work on a study site there, so his truck's two-seat cab was filled with gear, including a chainsaw. Tied into the truck bed was the canoe we'd paddle.

"The Geopoet," Richter said in greeting. We bumped fists. My admiration had only grown since I'd met him two years earlier during

Terry's "Friends of the Pleistocene" field weekend. I liked Richter because he performed rigorous soil science at a level both Albert and Hans Albert would recognize and admire, but also Richter saw his field as straddling many disciplines and he kept reading, consuming both classic and contemporary fiction and nonfiction. Richter's undergraduate philosophy degree showed through in everything he did. He was a humanist and scientist, crossed beautifully in a slim build, bald head, and agile mind. Since I'd seen Richter last, he seemed even more interdisciplinary than he was before. Richter said he had changed academic departments. He had instigated a deep dive into Appalachian literature and culture. He said that on the way down he'd listened to *Moby Dick*.

We swapped gear from Richter's truck to mine and drove a couple of miles upstream to the put-in. After forty years I still loved the mechanics of paddling trips, finding a put-in and take-out, "setting shuttle," untying gear, and "gearing up." It was one of the true, deep pleasures of my life, a ritual performed in order to meet the river on its own terms. There should be a little of a struggle. This was serious business.

As an earth scientist, Richter usually walks his study sites. We'd tried to visit the flume on an earlier scouting trip with Terry, but on that excursion, we were turned back from approaching it by a security guard at a self-storage complex that owns the access. The guard refused to let us pass, our goal only a hundred yards across a field to the river. That was when I proposed the river trip. Terry had planned to join us on this float trip but at the last moment something came up, so it was just Richter and me. Before we had left for Greenville on that first aborted scouting trip, Terry had contributed a set of drawings of the original structure that he'd found at the Library of Congress. With maps in hand, Richter and I were back, and I felt a little like an explorer.

The canoe was a short, green, fiberglass model, light, but, Richter quipped, quite tippy, and weightwise, we probably would overload it by fifty pounds. Richter told me as we drove to the put-in that he had inherited the vessel from his deceased father, who had bought it to paddle around a small lake he'd excavated on his property in New Jersey. Richter was determined to keep the boat in use. He said his father would be surprised to find us paddling it down the Enoree River in South Carolina.

I asked Richter what interested him about Einstein's Enoree River Observatory; he told me about how, even though he had grown up in New Jersey, he'd been attracted to southern landscapes since he was ten years old. "My attraction for forgotten places probably came from my mother," he said. "The Piedmont has so many forgotten sacred places." Richter left the mystery intact. He didn't attempt to explain what exactly makes a place sacred, but he knew this old ruin on the Enoree fit the bill. "The Piedmont, John, is well worth our time and study."

With the two of us being so vocationally different, it was unclear who should paddle in the stern and who in the bow. This was an especially important decision to make in a paddling relationship of any duration. As I reminded Richter, in the outfitter business the canoe was called "the divorce boat" because of all the disagreements that develop out of the hundred decisions one had to make navigating moving water. I thought for a moment of C. P. Snow's mythic "Two Cultures" and how putting a poet and scientist in the same canoe might be a toxic situation. But I knew that Richter's love of the arts and humanities and my reverence for field science would guide our way downstream. In the end, Richter sat in the front of the boat.

Once the canoe was secured below the put-in bridge, I clambered back up the riprap, locked the truck, and then descended again to meet Richter on the river side. I didn't know if Hans Albert had ever paddled the Enoree. I doubted it. It might have been a good place to do research, but maybe not so obvious as a spot for recreation. From where we stood, the Enoree didn't look like the kind of stream a non-river rat would want to drop a boat in, no pleasurable pond or bucolic backwater to paddle and float on a summer's day. Some might even demean the Enoree and dismiss it simply as a working-class industrial sluice or a big drainage ditch that never dried out. But for forty years I had been on a mission to get in touch with all the Piedmont rivers I could, and so when Richter was ready, we climbed in and pushed out from shore.

I was a little anxious to begin with. I worried we may have put on too late in the afternoon. But once afloat, any river felt like paradise: the traffic noise was dampened because you were usually below road level, the banks almost always were lined with trees, and even if you passed someone's backyard, most folks left the banks wooded. And there was, it seems, always wildlife on a river—deer or an ubiquitous great blue heron thirty yards ahead of the boat, or wood ducks leaving the shallows in pairs, their wings whistling.

But even though an argument about paradise could be made, I knew that a fall afternoon on a suburban Piedmont stream was not exactly Lewis and Clark or John Wesley Powell's scientific expedition down the Colorado in drift boats. But then again, I also knew when you were well past sixty, as both of us were, any day on the river could turn even a "three-hour tour" into a personal Corps of Discovery. It was best to stay vigilant about current and trees in the water and realize that disaster and success were always close cousins. So, with these two possible outcomes in mind—an idyllic paddle with a friend on a warm fall day to check off a historic spot in the upcountry's cultural history, or a disaster that could come at any moment from the collision of bad luck and unfamiliar water—I vowed to check the sun often so we could keep pace and get off the river by sundown. As Richter put it, when we took our first strokes, "This is important. Let's take good photos and write something that resounds!"

In October 1937, Hans Albert Einstein arrived in New York by ocean liner for a three-month scouting trip. His father Albert met him at the pier, and they posed for some photographs. The son playfully lit a long Dutch pipe he had brought as a gift for his father. On that trip Hans Albert drove across America with a friend so he could visit universities and seek work as an engineering professor. He drove ten thousand miles—Salt Lake City, Los Angeles, Iowa City, Knoxville, Vicksburg, Cleveland, Chicago, Detroit, and Indianapolis.

Albert Einstein's biographer reported that Albert wanted Hans to come to America so Albert could be closer to family. Albert's second wife had died, and he was all alone. But Hans Albert and his father had a problem. Albert didn't like Hans Albert's wife. Albert wrote to her a few times suggesting she not come on the trip to America with Hans. She didn't come. But after Albert had spent time with Hans, he relented and agreed to accept Hans Albert's wife. When Hans Albert left to return to Europe, Albert urged him to emigrate with his wife and their two children the following year and stay in America. They did come. This was how Hans Albert came to Greenville. He found employment in South Carolina with the Soil Conservation Service. Hans Albert's specialty was alluvial transport by rivers. He built a small brick house in Greenville, applied for American citizenship in December 1938, and settled into five years as a sediment researcher on the Enoree River.

In Greenville, there was one tragic moment. Hans Albert's wife was a Christian Scientist, and under her influence he became one as well. A few months after they arrived in Greenville, their six-year-old son, Klaus, contracted diphtheria. Because of their faith they refused medical assistance and he died. He was buried at the Woodlawn Cemetery in Greenville. This sad story pierced me when I first read it, since the boy was about the age I was when Daddy died, but this tragic reverse—parents losing a young child, rather than, in my case, the child left fatherless to make his way in the world.

After my first reading of the death, I'd thought often of the irony of the most famous scientist on the planet, one whose ideas were clearly at the heart of modernism, losing his grandson to an ancient disease and an almost medieval belief in God's power. "The deepest sorrow loving parents can experience has come upon you," Albert wrote to his son in a condolence note. Strangely, after the tragedy, Albert's relationship with his son became more secure. During the five years that Hans Albert lived in Greenville, Albert occasionally took the train south from Princeton to visit. In the afternoons, he would sometimes wander the roads and forests in or near town, often in dreamy thought spawning colorful anecdotes from astonished locals who helped him find his way home. I have always thought that Albert wandered Greenville's streets in bemusement, but maybe it was grief he was trying to walk away from. Was it the lost grandson that filled his mind on those visits?

The Enoree downstream from where we put in was narrow, deeply entrenched, and meandered back and forth through a mixed landscape of floodplain, north-facing bluffs, utility rights of way, and a sprawling patchwork of subdivision backyards that pinched in as close as they could to the wild river corridor.

On the upper stretch of the river there was good current when we had a reach of open water, but the paddling was unfortunately punctuated with brief portages and turned out to be a little more strenuous than I had planned. The narrow channel was sometimes blocked by deadfall logs in the first mile and a half downstream from the put-in. Often, we had to pull the canoe over. Then about a half mile along there was a rocky slide that was too shallow to paddle in our tippy little canoe. The footing was irregular enough, so we had to line the boat like Voyageur canoeists of old, bypassing rapids.

We soon passed through a power right-of-way and spooked a herd of eight or ten bedded does. As we approached, the does took off, leaping over brush matted down by the last high water, their white flags flying. Then a few more yards downstream, we spooked a lone big buck on the other side of the river, maybe the sultan of this panicked harem of even-toed ungulates. Time on a South Carolina river often rewards the paddler with such moments of imbedded wildness. Had we not disturbed them, these deer would be sequestered all day in river cane; at dusk they would wander a few hundred yards to eat the last green stems and ornamental flowers in the surrounding suburbs.

I wondered out loud how wild that spot would have been eighty years earlier when Hans Albert had worked downstream. Early scientists thought of all rivers as wild and untamed, some days calm as deer grazing in a meadow, others rampaging monsters. In the nineteenth century, there were no formulas for calculating either the flow rates or what the flow of streams might carry—gravel, sand, silt, and mud—as the velocities rose during and after a storm. The actions of a river were as mysterious as what might be happening inside the human body. But gradually, experiment after experiment, specialized researchers like Hans Albert began to plumb the depths of these natural systems and devise instruments for measuring them.

An hour along, we finally sighted the ruins of the research flume ahead of us. I was glad that a month earlier we had been denied permission to approach it by land through the industrial construction site and that I had hatched this paddling scheme instead—our only way to get to the site legally, though we would be trespassing once we stepped on shore.

I glanced at my phone, and the time was close to four. Sunset was at 5:18 p.m., so I was still a little concerned but wanted to make sure Richter had enough time to orient his thoughts to what was sketched out on the schema Terry had given us. It was close to time for Richter to ground-truth a few ideas about Hans Albert and his work there eighty years before.

I looked around. The sun was low to the West. I knew we had to negotiate the rocky, half-mile Gibbs Shoals before we reached our take-out at the Vietnamese Catholic church where Dan's truck was parked. We landed on a silt bar on river right, hard up against the tallest point on the cast concrete wall. After eighty years of neglect and weathering all the sluice's concrete superstructure didn't yet look like a natural part of the landscape. Concrete lasts a long time.

Ahead of us, the concrete walls on each side of the river funneled the current toward rows of parallel concrete fingers, the sluice itself. It sounded like a minor waterfall. All the bays were clogged by debris and almost covered over. The current seeped through where it could. Large upended oaks were caught against the upstream end. The sluice had been cast at the upper end of the shoals, so there were exposed boulders to contrast with the anthropogenic additions. I stood on the sediment bar and took notes and photos. Richter removed the schema from where I had stored it in my drybag and looked it over, said he could almost visualize all that happened here from the copy of the old black-and-white drawing. Richter stood a long time glancing at the drawing, then looked out at what was left of the research flume in the river. The flume was still quite impressive; it remained a powerful feature on the landscape. It was iconic, at least in our minds, and important to the fabric of things that matter to us, if not to the thousands who passed it every day a mile away on the interstate.

Richter climbed the wall above the river and tried to work out where all the station's superstructure had been. From his viewpoint he yelled down that most of it not in the river had been obliterated, probably bulldozed, and what was left had been buried in sediment. He walked about and then returned to report that one or two ruins protruded from the fill, enough to orient him on the schema. Not far inland from the riverside the storage company had leveled and filled a large pad for what looked like it could be a storage site. Development marches on, especially for those with access to heavy grading machinery.

I'd found a blog online where several local hydrologists had looked at the scs lab on the Enoree and figured out how it worked when it was in operation. They had observed how the concrete bays opened out into the riverbed. The individual slots, once opened, pumped water from each bay to a settling tank on the south side of the river. Here researchers like Hans Albert collected and weighed the sediment and determined its particle-size distribution. Then they returned the water to the river.

During its years of operation, from '38 until '42, the lab expanded what was known about sediment transport. Much of the research was Hans Albert Einstein's. The term "wash load" was even coined here. (Hydraulic engineers define wash load as the particles of sediment that move at different rates.) Besides walking around town, father Albert and son Hans would visit here and discuss engineering puzzles.

As the 1930s moved into the 1940s war era, the lab was abandoned as government priorities shifted to the engineering of more practical war needs. Most of the scientists associated with research in the Piedmont began moving to new positions. The deep soil research under way in the upper Piedmont began to move into a hibernation that would mostly last until thirty or forty years later. In 1942 Hans Albert moved his family to the Soil Conservation Service lab at Pasadena, California, and from there went on to a long and respected career in the science of sediment transportation. In a paper written for the 100th anniversary of Hans Albert's birth in 2004, two prominent contemporary hydrologists, Robert Ettema and Cornella F. Mutel, called Hans Albert "the archetypal researcher protagonist" determining "the way water flows."

Not only have I familiarized myself with what hydrologists think, I had also listened to Terry brief us about what he knew about the flume. He had explained how there was a problem with the Enoree river lab. The researchers couldn't control rainfall with concrete devices. The natural weather patterns of the Piedmont during the years of operation only produced enough rainfall in the watershed two to three times a year, and sometimes the flow was so great that they couldn't even measure it. Terry said of Hans Albert's work in the Enoree, "the flume was a failed experiment. It did not do what it was designed to do. Low flow the years it was installed made the river inadequate to do what he wanted to do. It was a very short-lived science project with a long footprint on the landscape."

There was one archetypal photo of Hans Albert knee-deep in the muddy waters of the Enoree taken during his years in Greenville. In one hand he controlled an apparatus he designed for measuring the way water flows. It looked suspiciously like an instrument he registered with the U.S. Patent Office in 1942. He wore a hat and rubber boots and held a staff; attached to it were what looked like multiple wine bottles with pipes protruding. The instrument disappeared below the river's surface, gathering data. Hans Albert looked intently at the river. You could tell by the little eddy forming behind his legs that the apparatus was pointed upstream, as I would suspect.

I stood on the sandbar taking notes as Richter climbed up and over the concrete retaining wall to ground-truth what was left above of the old research facility. Richter climbed through a break in the brush, and I peered across the river, blinded by the late sun slanting in from the West. When I looked up to where Richter had disappeared, I saw a figure. Was it Dan? It looked like Albert Einstein, more real than all the spirits of the Soil Conservation Service soil men I'd encountered at the gullies. Albert stood with his hands behind his back, his long hair swept off his forehead, wearing a quizzical expression. If the reports of his dress were correct, he was likely wearing bedroom slippers. He looked down at the river, lost in space and time—the physics of the moment collapsing his son's research site into calculations discussed at length, fluid dynamics, probability distributions, the movement of sediment, the complicated behavior of a river.

Standing there above me, Albert seemed oddly perplexed to be back. Maybe he remembered how he was the first to explain Brownian motion, a problem defined in 1837 of how in a drop of water observed in a microscope, dust, pollen, or a bit of sediment from a river moved around randomly, and how the particles looked like ants stirred up in an ant hill. According to Newtonian theory the particles should have sat motionless on the bottom of the droplet, but Albert explained their random motion, how they bumped into each other and set off in other directions—what physicists have called "the drunk man's walk."

Albert was just as comfortable with time as he was with sediment modeling, and that was where his mind likely settled. He was comfortable with the confounding reality of the universe, and fitting within it, the river flowing before him, a river his son was often knee-deep in. Albert understood all the human cultural systems of time—how to the western mind, time was segmented into precise, tiny units, scheduled, arranged, and managed; and how the Hindus thought it spiraled; and how to others it was what's called "polychronic," in that several events could happen at once. No culture was right about time and they all were, all at the same time.

What would Albert think of deep time? I'm sure he knew of James Hutton's famous eighteenth-century proclamation, that when we looked at the geological record there was "no vestiges of a beginning and no prospect of an end." Did Albert hear in Hutton an echo of his own mind?

If I had spoken to him, he would have reminded me that time was an illusion. Albert proved that with his famous theories. Time was relative, and it varied for different observers, depending on their speed through space. Richter and I had slowed down time on the river that day, floating downstream, paddle stroke after paddle stroke, sometimes not paddling at all, letting the river be our time machine. Albert caught the glint off the flowing current. He also saw the molecules bouncing through the river's narrowed bend as numbers in an equation. In his mind the real water and the ciphered water were one in the same.

Maybe some foreknowledge about this encounter with a spirit was part of the discomfort I felt upon embarkation. Maybe it wasn't my unease at knowing what could happen to us on the river if we were overtaken by nightfall after all. There is no easy way to consort with spirits. I remembered my reading of *The Odyssey* and how Odysseus poured out a drink of blood for the ghost of Achilles on the shore of the Styx. I didn't have any libations with me except for a bottle of water. I wished for a moment I had at least brought some gorp.

Before my reverie ended, I saw yet another spirit standing with Albert, looking down at me, a small boy in a dark sweater, about the age I was when Daddy died in Southern Pines. His body could have been woven of black gauze. The two figures on the shore side by side seemed united in time or space, and somehow, I was with them too. Was this Klaus? I was sure Hans Albert brought his son to play by the river while he worked. A father would do that. Did he also visit here with his famous grandfather down from Princeton? This question seemed silly to contemplate in an audience with a spirit. What question should I have asked of the dead? Maybe I should not have even asked a question. Maybe I should have comforted the grandfather and mourned the passing of the boy. The pain of loss was still palpable around them. The pain of Klaus's early death was the gauzy film around his body. Before I could formulate another line of inquiry the spirits vanished, and the space once energized was just an open patch of blue sky above me.

I didn't doubt what I'd seen or felt. Here next to the Enoree it could have been the nineteenth century, or it could have been 1941, or it could have been the present. The cast concrete seemed immortal, the color of human flesh, but much more durable in the passing of time. Einstein did not deny entropy, though he rearranged our concepts of time. Then someone spoke. It was Richter calling to our little narrow shelf of time. It was not the Einsteins, dead for decades. But if there were spirits about, surely, they were present in a spot like that where the immortal could walk and the river pass.

Richter worked his way back down over the concrete wall, and I kept my séance with Albert to myself. It was my little field trip secret. We waded into the river and passed the canoe through one of the clogged bays in the flume. The water was two feet deep on the slightly sloping concrete pad under the whole structure, and we had good footing for working with the canoe. Richter stood in the bay next to where I passed the canoe along. He banged his paddle on the concrete flooring where it must have been hollow beneath because it rang out with a ghostly music.

Bedrock

The substructure composed of hard rock exposed or buried at the earth's surface; an exposed portion of bedrock is often called an outcrop.

OLD WOODLAND
Little or no erosion

ABANDONED CROPLAND
Severe sheet erosion
Remnant of topsoil held by tree

Gully
tough
and c
in rot
C ho

A horizon

Severe sheet erosion and
shallow gullying in B horizon

ROTTEN   WEATHERED   ROCK

Deep
Gully

ROTTEN   ROCK

SOLID   BEDROCK
GRANITE GNEISS

Mary Brown Lane, Johnny Lane, Herbert O'Shields, and
Infant Sean Camby, on a Stoop of Briarcliff Road, Spartanburg, S.C.
(Sandra Alverson Camby, 1968)

Briarcliff Road

Mama got sober, but it took a long time. Her longtime boyfriend Herbert bought her the white-shingled, Cape Cod–style house on Briarcliff Road in 1967, but Mama always claimed she made the house payments. How? Sandy's not sure. We always lived month to month on government benefits after we came back to Spartanburg—from Daddy's Social Security and VA checks. When Mama died, we discovered plenty of paperwork about how she worked out the financial puzzles of her life. She figured things out on legal pads mostly, listing her monthly bills in a column, then subtracting each from her bank balance, always walking on a financial edge. Owning the house on Briarcliff Road must have finally felt like a redemption for her.

When we moved to Spartanburg, my sister was my only familiar childhood lifeline besides neighborhood friends, who were always changing, because we moved so much. In those years sports were my steady pastime. As a teenager, I played football and basketball. And there was my banana seat bicycle I rode until I got my first car, a Carolina blue '65 Ford Falcon Herbert bought for $500. I used the car on my paper route through the neighborhood. Mama rolled the papers every morning, then woke me, and I went out to throw them.

Sandy had a series of boyfriends in high school and afterward. That was her way out. Did she think of herself as wild back then? "Yes, I was wild and free, and could pretty much do as I pleased," she told me. Even after Sandy married in 1965, when I was eleven, she always kept tabs on me. She came over to eat lunch or to see Mama and me two or three times a week. Don, the man Sandy married when she was nineteen, was five years older than she was, and he worked at a loom factory in town called Draper. Once Sandy was married, we became closer, or, at least, I leaned more on her. I spent a great deal of time with Don's family in Pacolet. His family was still working in the mill at that time, and they lived on a rural road surrounded by gullied red clay fields of rabbit tobacco and golden broom sedge in the fall. I remember Don's father had that hardscrabble face you see often in Spartanburg County—my people—with a stubble of beard. I always picture him in overalls. Don had two younger brothers. The youngest brother hunted rabbits and squirrels with a .410 shotgun and took me along. Don's mother was the closest thing I remember to a grandmother. She doted on her boys and cooked the standard proletarian fare of the Piedmont back then, heavy on biscuits and fatback—adding fried squirrel and rabbit when we brought it in. I remember her voice sounding like a dripping spring except when they started yelling. "It was a trait of his family. They had to yell to be heard," Sandy remembered, laughing.

Family was a big part of my survival in those years. Once, talking with Betsy, the subject of kin came up, first cousins in particular. She has two, one dead and one living. I had to call Sandy to calculate a workable inventory of my own on my mother's side. I counted what I could but knew I'd come up way short. Sandy counted off twenty-nine from the various marriages of my grandmother Hulda. But hairsplitters in the genealogy world might quibble and call some of these cousins "half first cousins."

I don't know how the family gatherings fit in with Mama's drinking in those years. Once we were in Spartanburg the drinking intensified though. Was it grief for her dead husband John and her lost settled life on Ashe Street in Southern Pines—our own house, two cars, a husband with a decent job gone down the drain of neglect? Or was it the illness of her addiction, already eroding any hope of her living a normal life until she found some sort of workable treatment, which would be years later?

For a while, I thought I might move in with Sandy and Don down at Pacolet. I often wonder how my life would have changed if my high school years had been spent down there in rural Spartanburg County. Pacolet High was mostly white and (primarily) poor. Spartanburg High was urban, the largest school in the state, a rich ecosystem of multiple classes and races. Years later I asked a guidance counselor I knew who had worked in both districts (Spartanburg and Pacolet) what the differences were in the student populations. He said at Spartanburg the intellectual curve had a big high end and a big low end and no middle. "Down there it's almost all middle."

Intellectually, at that time, I was certainly more comfortable in that middle. I didn't read much. I hadn't started asking big questions like I did later in high school, and I didn't really aspire toward much either. No one would have ever called me "gifted" as a student back then and I limped along. I drifted through academically and this continued until I was in college.

But in the end, I didn't go down to Pacolet. I stayed in Spartanburg and my life became increasingly compartmentalized. I had a life and I had home. I made friends. I climbed socially. I played sports. There were gullies—in those years, particularly Mama's drinking and poverty—but I somehow stayed back from the edge. I made up my own story. When someone asked me why Daddy was missing, I said he'd "died of a heart attack." I couldn't say the word "suicide." When friends asked to come home with me to hang out, I made excuses, afraid we would find my mother passed out in her bedroom.

In '68, the summer after Herbert bought Mama the house, we stayed at a riverside cabin at Chimney Rock Park in the North Carolina mountains for a week. Sandy has a picture of me wearing a madras hat, white tee shirt, and Bermuda shorts. It was the only time I saw Herbert with his shirt off. He had a thick, white, pasty chest and a farmer's tan. He wore long dress pants and dress shoes. There was a boy on the river that summer who killed water snakes with a bull whip, snapped their heads off as they sunned. Herbert bought me a bull whip at the tourist store, but I never wanted to pop heads off snakes.

Mama's attempts at employment through those years were always spotty. After moving to Spartanburg, she worked for a while as a hostess at Howard Johnson's restaurant. That was where she met Herbert. Later she was paid to sit with an elderly neighbor next door. Then she worked a little job as a clerk at a place called the Remnant Shop.

Neither Sandy nor I could ever remember her longing for more. She was happy to cook and sew for her family. There was one attempt to sell her services as a home seamstress, but she never made much money from that. She made a flyer to hand out at the Mental Health Clinic where she went for treatment for years. It hangs above my desk: "NOTICE Will do sewing in my house. Ladies and childrens garments. REASONABLE PRICES."

Herbert was our stability but he was a philanderer. He was the cliché of the traveling salesman. There was always another woman somewhere on the furniture sales route. He never married Mama, even after his ill wife passed away in 1965. He and Mama had a long relationship—twenty years—and that helped close the absence left by my daddy's death. Herbert did sacrifice for us though. Mama never would have owned that house on Briarcliff Road if Herbert hadn't taken out the mortgage. Her credit was shot.

When Mama was drunk Herbert would bring her a box containing a take-out sliced pork sandwich and onion rings from the Beacon Drive-In, the fast food place down the road, but he also brought her whiskey. Though he didn't drink himself, Herbert justified bringing Mama bottles because, he said, that way, she wouldn't drive herself or call a cab. Cab drivers were the worst. Sometimes they'd steal her money or even come inside with her. When she drank Herbert often yelled at her and she'd cry and plead, saying, "One more pint and I'll never drink again." The promise was good only until the checks came the next month.

Mama was a binge drinker and went on alcoholic tears. Before she'd left Southern Pines, she'd joined AA, but it didn't stick. She would drink like she baked—in a fury. The checks would arrive on the first of the month and set her off. She'd drink for a week, run out of money, and then not drink again until the next set of government checks arrived. The weeks Mama drank she passed out in her bedroom. I worried she'd burn the house down. Her mattress was a cratered field of cigarette holes from smoking in bed. When her drinking was at its worst, we threatened to send her "to Bull Street," the South Carolina asylum in Columbia. Maybe it was Herbert who started that. I don't know. It's one of the things I still feel most guilty about from those difficult years.

Mama had a complicated relationship with organized religion. When she drank, she called preachers of all denominations and confessed her recent sins with the bottle. Once she called Billy Graham. I can still hear the rising strands of "Blessed Assurance" as sung on the television by George Beverly Shea. After the altar call a crusade hotline appeared on the screen, and she tried it. Billy Graham actually called her back, but it did not save her from despair, and the next month when the government checks came, she sinned again. On Mama's bedroom wall she displayed a painting of an old-time baptism, a dunking in a red mud Piedmont river. She said it amused her to glance up at that picture and remember she'd been "baptized once and sprinkled twice, and none of them took."

She always hid her liquor bottles when she binged, but for the most part, she wasn't very creative. We'd find them under the kitchen sink, and there would be a shot glass turned upside down on the drain board. That's the first thing I looked for in the kitchen. That was the sign of a binge approaching, like a storm, and it meant a full week of TV dinners and skipping school. In spite of the incentives, I poured the bottles of cheap Schenley's down the kitchen sink when I found them.

The three weeks every month Mama was sober Herbert watched TV with us at night before he'd go home. Those were the years of protest and civil rights on the news with Walter Cronkite. Herbert was always on the wrong side. He had a good streak but was definitely a man of his time and place. His favorite TV show was *All in the Family*, and he laughed when Archie Bunker called his son-in-law "the meathead."

Maybe Herbert was clairvoyant and knew I would become a writer, because when he saw me reading *Look Homeward, Angel* in junior high, he drove me over to meet Thomas Wolfe's brother Fred, who lived in the fancy neighborhood on the east side of town. Fred (Luke in the novel) sold ice cream downtown for Blue Bird and Herbert had met him there.

Though no reader, Herbert was a storyteller. He'd spin yarns from farm life in Pauline, in southern Spartanburg County, not far from where one of Terry's gullies was. There were stories about the Depression, cold winters, rabbit hunting, revivals, and stump meetings. He also told stories of his drives through Spartanburg County collecting payments for furniture, always leaving out the important part about the extra women. These stories brought the county to life, and I loved the names of the places he collected from—New Prospect, Cooley Springs, Fingerville, Sugar Tit. These were some of the gifts he gave me, as well as a .22 rifle, a box of quilts his grandmother made, and an old black baseball glove with broken leather sinews that once held the fingers together.

He loved boxing too, though mostly he liked to tell me about the old heavyweight champions—Jack Dempsey, Joe Lewis, Rocky Marciano. Herbert took me to shake hands with the retired undefeated champion Rocky Marciano when he made an appearance promoting Azalea meats at a new BI-LO on Whitney Road. Rocky had big hands, or maybe it was just that mine were so small. Herbert hated Muhammad Ali though and always insisted on calling him "Cassius Clay." Sometime in the mid-1960s we went to see a live boxing match at Spartanburg Memorial Auditorium, and the city's most famous boxer, Pappy Gault, was in attendance. Gault was a bantamweight and stood five feet three, not much taller than I was at the time. He'd been retired ten years by then, but Herbert made sure I knew how good he'd been. He'd won the National Golden Gloves title, been the alternate for the Olympics in '48, and won the North American bantamweight title in '52. Gault liked to gamble, and in '71 he and another man were shot and killed after a poker game. One Christmas, Herbert bought me boxing gloves, and an older neighborhood boy suckered me into dropping my guard. He said he wouldn't hit me in the face, but sucker punched me, knocked me out. That was the end of my brief boxing career.

Herbert showed a romantic side Mama liked. One night he took her out to the end of the runway at the downtown airport, just like the soldier had done during the war. She told us about it later. He turned her head side to side. "Herbert, what are you doing?" she asked.

"I just like to see how your face looks in the moonlight," he answered.

Another time, Herbert drove Mama and me to a high spot above Spartanburg's first shopping center, called Pinewood. He wanted us to see the lights of the parking lot come on after dusk. It must have been a sight to behold for that Spartanburg country boy turned furniture salesman.

Mama quit drinking in the 1980s. In April of '82 she went to the emergency room and was admitted. After Mama passed away, Sandy showed me her medical records. The report describes her as an "alert, somewhat anxious white female." She was experiencing nausea and had a medical history suggesting internal bleeding. Sandy said when Mama checked in, she had "hemoglobin of 4.1 grams when normal is at least 12.0." The years of alcohol had finally taken their toll internally. The tests showed she had an ulcer and almost bled out. The doctors told her if she ever drank again it would kill her.

She didn't take a drink for the last twenty years of her life.

About the time Mama stopped drinking, she couldn't take Herbert's constant girlfriends anymore. He had one named Peaches who lived on Cannon's Campground Road. Mama found out about her and would drive out and cruise past the house. They even talked to each other on the phone, just two women comparing notes on their cheating man. Herbert's last girlfriend was named Sandy, and that was Mama's last straw. Mama asked him not to come back. Before he left, Herbert agreed to sign the house over to us in order for Mama to continue living in the only house she knew. Later he married a much younger woman, but she left him when he got older. Herbert died penniless in 2000, alone at eighty-five in a downtown apartment building.

In spite of the drinking and the pain that must have come from Herbert's philandering, that house on Briarcliff was better for Mama. It had functioned like a port in a long storm. She rode out the bad years, and she enjoyed the good ones. Aunts, uncles, cousins, and friends gathered there because Mama loved to cook and bake, especially around holiday time. She would get on a kick, things she'd gleaned maybe from *Southern Living* or the Sunday newspaper. She made dark-brown, sticky-date nut bread baked in tin cans with the bottoms and tops cut out. There was a fruit cake era, and banana pudding, pound cake, and pecan pie were all baked, holidays or not.

Another of Mama's routes to recovery was sewing. Before Daddy died, Sandy remembered Mama driving from Southern Pines to Rockingham to buy her first sewing machine—a Singer. Sandy remembered that Mama sewed for her dance recitals. Mama sewed on that old Singer until she bought a new one in the early 1970s. The new machine had a beige plastic cover, and it was a presence that always sat on a little desk in her bedroom, waiting with its needle and spools of thread. Mama kept it tuned up, oiled, cleaned. "I think it's still out in our storage shed," Sandy said.

There were always stacks of patterns in the bedroom next to the Singer. Mama made clothes for Sandy, Sandy's husband, her grandchildren, Sandy's son's wife, and the two great-grandkids, and even a few things for me. She was better with women's clothing than with men's. She once surprised me with a maroon, double-breasted sportscoat with big, gold buttons to wear to my ninth-grade sports banquet. I wore that coat once, and it hung in the front closet for thirty years until we threw it out after her death when we cleaned out the house. The last things Mama sewed were Raggedy Ann and Andy dolls and baby clothes for Sean and Kim's two girls.

It's obvious there's a lot I would like to forget about those years. There was also plenty to remember. I became who I am during the years on Briarcliff Road. If I have an identity, the core of it was formed there—the storyteller listening around the dinner table, the high school boy who keeps his friends at a distance from his home, the fatherless boy engaged with the older man who loves his mother but never marries her.

The house on Briarcliff Road has been gone for twenty years, sold by us to a Methodist church demolished after Mama died. Sometimes I think of something that hasn't surfaced for a long time. "There was that round metal thing in the backyard," I said to Sandy as we compared notes about Briarcliff Road. She didn't know what I was talking about. Sandy had never lived on Briarcliff, except for a brief period when her husband Don was going to college in Columbia. She spent very little time in the backyard. "I was out there every day for years, mostly pounding down the grass at the basketball hoop Herbert built for me," I said. "I was fascinated with that round metal thing." Our neighbors didn't know what the object was, either, or how it came to be in our backyard.

The thing was about three feet tall, round topped, with five mysterious holes and a rusted patina. It stood in one corner of the yard shadowed by oaks. I showed Sandy a picture I found online of an object just like it. "It's a nautical capstan," I said. "For multiplying the pulling force for hauling ropes and cables, like for pulling up an anchor." She looked puzzled. "I've been thinking about how this thing was us telling a story."

"How?" she asked.

"You know, hauling up difficult weighty deposits from the depths," I said, laughing.

The house had been built in 1945, which maybe gave us a clue about the capstan. Maybe its previous owner was a returning veteran who somehow hauled the relic inland and sunk the base in concrete. Or maybe it came from a sunken ship, one scrapped for salvage once the war ended. Whatever the story, somebody went to a great deal of trouble to plant it on Briarcliff Road. As a boy the mystery object taught me how to leapfrog, a skill I sometimes practice to this day.

Real Estate Sign, Fingerville, S.C. (John Lane, 2019)

Alverson Gully

The Alverson Gully was a green slash through loosely rooted water oaks, a gnarly kudzu-clogged wound on the land. Terry and I stood on the gully lip and stared in. This time we planned to do some fieldwork. Dan Richter was driving down from Duke. He would meet up with us, as Terry had a number of gully stops to make.

It was deep summer. I remembered that in winter, when the kudzu was dead, we could actually see the bottom. Now the kudzu filled it up. Despite that, this spot had deep implications for our family story. After three years of searching I could no longer claim our family was an underground stream hidden from my eyes. They were real people now. They were a filled-out line standing side by side, shoulder to shoulder, way back into the Piedmont past. I was connected to them through the serious genealogical research of my sister, the hard data of DNA tests, and the softer sinews of story.

What good could a gully possibly be? Not much if you were concerned with putting in a crop of cotton, planting a peach orchard, grazing animals, building a home place, or looking for level industrial land to lay out a plant or a subdivision. The only real upside of gullies is that they were very good at growing kudzu. They are also of literary and scientific value. A gully is a window into what's below or to the side. For the soil scientist, dramatic erosion opens up seams through the land and lets them walk through. For a storyteller, gullies are good for metaphor. They point to deeper themes. They free up territory for beauty, understanding, and occasional terror.

The Alverson Gully could have been one of the gullies where Sauer visited and sampled on his 1936 southern field trip. That was definitely one of the gullies where the early researchers found the Pleistocene-age buried organic deposits that had dogged this story from near the beginning. In the scientific literature the Alverson Gully took its place alongside many other Piedmont gullies to elucidate the natural landscape that Sauer loved, and, as data, possibly would contribute to reconceptualizing Piedmont geology. That was, if Terry and Richter could write a few world-class papers.

As we walked back from the gully lip to the Fingerville church parking lot where the truck was, Terry reminded me how Sauer defined a landscape, as a "distinct association of forms, both physical and cultural." I reminded him that Sauer's definition had been sleeping within me for forty-five years since I first read it as a young poet in Port Townsend, Washington. "It's as if that early reading was in preparation for this visit to this landscape," I said.

What made this a story for me, though, was the family connection, the part Sauer would call "the cultural landscape." Highway 11 was no wilderness. The mountains loomed close, almost shadowing us, but these mountains had a soft, inviting blue hue. As far as we could see, this was a landscape that had been utilized by human beings for thousands of years. I knew my people had done their part. On my first trip to the Alverson Gully, my sister had reminded me that within a mile of where we stood survived the house where our great-great-grandfather Columbus Christopher Bradley lived and tenant farmed in the late 1910s. He had died there. Another three miles down Highway 11 and we could pass where my nephew Sean and his wife Kim had recently built a house and lived. A couple of miles in the other direction and we would pass the Fingerville textile mill village. Our relatives never worked there, but plenty of them worked and lived in a half dozen similar mill villages like it in Spartanburg County.

So, there was a strong connection between land and life in northern Spartanburg County along Highway 11. Ten thousand years ago early hunter-gatherers moved up from the coast to the foothills and mountains in the spring along the abundant southeast-running rivers and streams—the Pacolet, Buck Creek, Shoaly Creek—and worked back downstream in the fall. They might have stood on this high, clear hilltop and looked toward what we now call White Oak

Mountain, a distinct geologic landmark on the rising Appalachian front. I tended to run too deep into nostalgia and prefer one imagined cultural landscape over another. I felt the strong waves of empathy sweeping over me as I thought about those hunter-gatherers four hundred generations in the past. I spiraled into a vision of men and women making their way through old-growth hardwoods they are intimate with, beside clear streams, sleeping in rock shelters, and hunting abundant familiar game. There was an accompanying woodwind soundtrack like the twittering of retreating birds.

I privileged the imagined lives of these people over our strong Bradley forebears who worked this land or their children who moved into the textile mills. I felt a bit guilty and embarrassed about this bias. This excavation, which Terry and my sister had led me on, had tempered my bias for the deep past. My reveries didn't last as long as they once did. Maybe I'd always used the deep past as an excuse to blunt my disappointment in the present. What would Harrington say about that? In spite of my occasional consorting with spirits, Harrington didn't appear to answer my question, but I did have, "live-and-in-person," Terry Ferguson.

"You've escaped one time trap, but you've fallen into another one," Terry said, after hearing me out. "You have the ability to become unstuck in time and you can see the natural and human landscapes. But you want to find a direct and transcendent interaction with the landscapes, which was another time trap. It's just like your desire to find the wilderness." Terry looked toward the mountains. "You want to imagine an untouched world, even though this world has been touched many times. These hunter-gatherers were human. They had their own desires and biases, just like you and your Bradleys."

Back in the present, I looked around and began once again to inventory. From our perch on the tailgate of the truck it was possible to see there had been some major changes at the site of the Alverson Gully since Terry and I were last here. Two years earlier there had been a sign and a few houses, but a subdivision was now fully under way called "Alverson Farms." The sign informed us the site was 46.5 acres. So far, all that was built were houses ("starting at $150K") west along the south side of Rainbow Lake Road. The sign suggested there was more to come with plans for extensive construction on the vacant land. On the way up Rainbow Lake Road we'd turned down a road into a little subdivision named "Bent River." Was it named after a sharp bend in the Pacolet River that flows nearby, now dammed for Spartanburg's water supply?

"Until the 1950s half the Piedmont was under cultivation," Terry mused of the loss. "Now it's probably less than 10 percent, and many of these old fields first were converted to silviculture—plantation forests, tree farms—and now they're moving to subdivisions."

"Smurf houses," I said, with no lack of privileged scorn, then chuckled, thinking about my own biases again.

"Well, this construction will be bad for science," Terry added, then reminded me how the Alverson Gully fronts on the highway. "We need to get in there and auger before the developer fills that gully for more road-front lots."

Soon Richter arrived. He greeted us warmly, as always, with salutations. I wondered what magical literature he had listened to on the way down from Durham. More *Moby Dick*? Maybe Bronte, or Darwin? Or was he listening to Bach?

Richter stood by and Terry briefed him on the gullies we would try to locate. Terry showed Richter more old documents he'd recovered—going back to the 1930s work. I asked Richter and Terry, "What percentage of active earth scientists use this sort of mining of old data?"

"Way too little," Richter said. "If you hand out something from the 1930s in class a student will always ask, 'Why aren't we reading real science?' They want literature that's right up-to-date."

"Yes, only a few scientists would be interested in this," Terry added. "I sent a young scientist an article about this project written in 1937. He didn't understand why I had sent it to him."

After this discussion we loaded ourselves into Terry's truck and drove up a dead-end road angling off Highway 11 to show Richter the Alverson house, but soon enough we saw that it was gone! The cultural landscape had been stripped of one beautiful data set. I flipped through my phone photos and showed Richter what it had looked like on the hilltop two years earlier. "At that time there was actually somebody living here," I said. Now the resident and the house had both vanished. Even the foundation had been bulldozed and cleared. Grass had grown over the scar. All that remained were several of the large oaks that shaded the house, but they too would probably be cleared in what contemporary developers call "cut and scrape" housing construction. In that construction paradigm, trees and hills were merely impediments to be neutralized by heavy machinery. A flat building site improved the balance sheet and trees could easily be replaced. Whoever would purchase the lot where the "Alverson Farm" house stood would have only a vague notion of who the Alversons were, or what they farmed. This farm would always be given quotation marks. I felt bad for Sandy. One more page of Alverson material history had now been erased and written over with a new subdivision. The house occupied by her second cousin two times removed had officially ceased to exist. We were now officially growing houses in the old Alverson cotton fields.

"But that too is part of the cultural landscape," I said, mostly to myself, correcting my biases as I went.

I texted Sandy the sad news about the old Alverson farmhouse, and I asked for directions to the other house of our own blood kin, our great-great-grandfather Columbus Christopher Bradley. Where did he live on Highway 11 and in what year? Sandy texted directions to the house right back. She told me years earlier she'd made a trip up to find it. "A two-story farmhouse called the Old Johnson Place," she texted back. Then she sent another text, reminding me of information she'd told me many times: "B 1856 Rutherford County D, 1920 New Prospect." I knew that New Prospect was a few miles southwest. Not so far. This was indeed a corridor rich in our family history. New Prospect. What a great name; I'd always loved it. And, I took great pride that I'd had a relative die in such a place. I was the long-down-the-line "new prospect" Columbus Christopher Bradley would never have anticipated, "a storyteller" in his direct line, shaping his ancestors' hardscrabble life into a tale.

Before we continued the hard-science expedition, I asked Terry and Richter to tolerate my cultural excursion. Would they drop me at "the old Johnson place" where Columbus Christopher Bradley lived in 1920? I wanted to commune a little with the diverse spirits of my ancestors. Maybe I'd sense something around the place. Of course, they would take me there, they said, both being scientists of broad interests and easily triggered curiosity.

"We roam the world looking for a blessing," a friend once told me. Would I get one?

There it was again—curiosity. It was close to paying off. I was ready to follow past the threshold into personal understanding. If I could stand in the yard where Columbus Christopher Bradley stood, I might just know something deeper about myself. I might get a good look at how far I had come from that gully-addled boy only three years removed from his father's suicide. I was a man who had pushed through and was now sixty-six years old. I'd done okay for myself. My friendships with Terry and Richter showed me that. They were both good men with fierce, caring minds. I might not score highly on the math SAT as they likely did, but I could hang with their insights and even create my own.

John Harrington believed every student was one question away from genius. Geology was the vessel he chose to serve communion. In what other discipline could you feel that way?

"Everybody has insight," Terry said he remembered Harrington saying. "The goal is to create enough understanding so that you can see how your world works."

I may not have been the smartest cat on the deck railing, but I was often the one with the most curiosity. I liked to think that's why Harrington singled me out of the horde of football players and econ majors on the lab bus and told me, "Go write poetry, lad." And that I did. So how did curiosity translate to that day on the road to

Fingerville? How could I open up to it? How did I avoid fear and lean toward curiosity? How could I elucidate that moment so we can all share it? If we were to get through it, then we must all see the world in our own grains of sands. We must all walk forward into our own eternities.

We continued west on Highway 11. We passed the gully on the Alverson property, and Richter related how he had come here on his own once, done some probing, and found buried organic deposits, so it was definitely a good place to reinvestigate. I was jealous for a moment. I'd yet to lay eyes on the buried organic deposits. They were nothing but reported data. Sometimes I doubted that they existed at all. But I wasn't unhappy. The idea of buried organic deposits had served me well as metaphor: the carbon remnants of life buried under great weight and pressure for eons. When recovered, yielding so much information. The excavation and the lab work were everything. Running the pollen, keeping strict numbers on depth from surface. My sister Sandy knew that from her years of genealogy just as well as the scientists Terry and Richter knew it. I'd learned it too.

Navigating by texted directions from Sandy, we drove to where Prison Camp Road intersected Halls Bridge Road. Initially we proceeded down Prison Camp Road a short distance, a misdirection on my part, but a profitable one. On our left some landowner had posted a sign on a gully asking for fill—concrete, bricks, dirt, hoping to make level land out of what was low and unproductive. That sign allowed me to contemplate the fate of Piedmont gullies. Gullies were not well loved, but here we were seeking them out, working them for data and enlightenment.

Over twenty years ago Sandy first revealed to me what she knew about the complexity of the census records, and Columbus Christopher Bradley's story lit me up—from mulatto or Indian to white in forty years. I called him "Christopher Columbus" back then, appropriate for that long-lost "Indian ancestor." I liked the irony of the name. I built a whole mythology around the family's Indian origins—how the family name was maybe originally, "Broadleaf," and the other branches feeding off and into the Bradley branch had names like "Bee Healer" and "Panther." When Sandy later discovered that C. C. stood for "Columbus Christopher," not "Christopher Columbus," of course I was disappointed. Mythology never proved simple when examined.

Columbus Christopher Bradley was the best documented of the first few generations of Bradleys. Sandy had extensive census records, plus interviews with cousins and aunts, several of whom remembered him. There also were good photos of him. One showed his big family, while he was sitting there front and center with a moustache and a hat. His eyes looked dark. In another he sat in a stiff-back chair with big, dark hands holding on to his knees as if that's where the family's secrets resided.

A great aunt once told Sandy a story. When the aunt was maybe four or five—she was born in 1904—her family took a trip to Atlanta to see the Bradley cousins. From New Prospect to Atlanta would have been a long road trip back then—maybe two hundred hilly miles. Maybe they caught a ride with someone who already owned a car, driving the old Atlanta Road through Spartanburg, through Greenville, Anderson, and across the Savannah River into Georgia; maybe they rode a wagon twenty miles southeast to Spartanburg's Union Station and caught the train there, with stops every ten miles or so—Wellford, Vernonville, Greer's Depot, Chick Springs, Greenville Court House, Pickensville, Liberty, Centre, Keowee, Seneca, Cedar Mountain, Westminster, and Horseshoe, all before they crossed the river.

I'm guessing they took the train. If so, they arrived in Atlanta and caught a streetcar out to the Grant Park neighborhood near the entrance to the Atlanta Zoo, where the Bradley cousins lived. The cousins were textile workers, moved to Georgia from South Carolina. Who went? We can only speculate. What time of year was it? Perhaps winter, when there was time to travel with no crops to keep. The old aunt remembered that on the visit to Atlanta somebody taught her how to crochet. I liked this story because I thought it showed Columbus Christopher breaking out, how his was the first generation of an expanding world for the Bradley line. Suddenly, about that time the cultural landscape of our kin opened up a great deal. It didn't look so unlikely to get from there to here.

We doubled back to see the 1870 farmhouse still standing, the one where Columbus Christopher Bradley died in 1920. It was from this house where he tenant-farmed and launched his brood of children, the oldest being our great-grandfather John Simeon Bradley. Columbus Christopher Bradley didn't know it at the time, but from here he assured his story would be told.

The house was much bigger than I expected. It was two stories, set back off the road among mature pecan trees and one very large red oak. I expected a shotgun tenant house with three or four rooms at most, and no underpinning. But that white house was grand. That rented ancestral house had real presence. There were nice chimneys on each end, half fieldstone and half brick, a big front porch, some architectural flourishes, like dental trim under the gables, and scalloped shingles as siding over a first-story big bay window. The house definitely had been upgraded some, likely after my people lived there.

I surveyed the yard and wondered what it would have been like in 1920 when Columbus Christopher Bradley lived there. His tenant farm was now in the midst of a dramatic revision, from remnant agricultural landscape to sprawl, from rural to something approaching the outer edge of metro—the expansion of the edge of Spartanburg north. The Bradleys were part of another transformation, from early twentieth century small hill farms to cotton mills. Columbus Christopher Bradley plowed until he died, though just a generation later, none of his children farmed. Many of them worked the mill, though others were domestics, and one a fuel truck driver.

Was that falling-down wellhouse here in 1920? That old barn? The big oak? The pecans? The pecan trees were mature, but they grow pretty fast. I zeroed in on the oak. It became my connection to Columbus Christopher Bradley, the last of the farming line of Bradleys before his sons went off to the mills. He was my most complex and familiar ancient touchstone. I could feel it standing there. He always had been familiar to me. Maybe it was because we had good photos of him, taken always in his best clothes.

A thin place was said to be where distance between heaven and earth collapse, where we might catch a glimpse of eternity. But my great-great-grandfather's tenant farm didn't feel thin. Eternity felt thick there. The topsoil of human context was deep and familiar and had not easily eroded, even after neglect or abandonment. But rather than eternal I felt young again standing in that yard. There was no way I was older than C. C. Bradley was when he died here at sixty-four. Every object around me glowed with possibility. Every space was familiar. Around me in the farmyard I saw doorways open downward into my own past. I was not talking about geologic time. I was glad Harrington taught me about that. I was glad to have experienced a youthful conversion to deep time, but deep time required even deeper faith. After forty-five years it was still a hard concept to grasp and hold onto. I was talking about time that was way more familiar—time and events I could commune with.

I didn't summon a spirit as I did with Richter on the Enoree, but I did feel my people there. That farmyard was the material argument for their presence I'd been searching for. The salt residue of their bodies still rested in the fallow fields beyond the house. Somewhere were buried the bones of their old mule. Somewhere else, lay the exfoliating iron husk of Columbus Christopher Bradley's hoe. They lived and worked there. Their story took root in that very ground.

I knocked on the front door and a gray-haired woman in a plaid dress answered. She eyed me a little suspiciously but warmed up when I told her my great-great-grandfather died in that house in 1920. She said she wouldn't know anything about that. They'd bought the house from a Miss Gilbert in 1970. "She raised thirteen children here," she said.

"Do you farm?" I asked.

"No, but this house was surrounded by peach orchards when we moved. They're all gone now."

We drove five more miles on Highway 11 to check out the final gullies of the day. We cruised through Cooley Springs, still an oasis of Piedmont agriculture, with hundreds of acres of peach trees. Bright pink peaches littered the ground, fruit fallen from the trees, unharvested. Right next to this orchard was an open field with dirt so red it looked like a bloody hill. Men worked with survey equipment there to lay out perfect rows of new, young trees. I asked about the soil and Richter said, "It's the Cecil," the most common soil in the Piedmont, a clay, rich in iron, over a million acres. "It's the official soil of North Carolina. A soil always with a diminutive A horizon. It's been beheaded, decapitated. In the Duke Forest we've shown that erosion removed twenty inches (50 cm) of topsoil. But the eighty years of trees there has regenerated some of it, building back at least a B horizon." Looking at the blood red Cecil I thought of my own family's struggles farming in the Piedmont, my blood, all the loss, all the heartache. What would bedrock be to a human being?

We inspected the Cooley Gully at a stream crossing where barn swallows floated in and out from under the bridge. Then we piled back in Terry's truck and turned up a small road in search of the original Sauer gully. Where did Terry think the gully might be? In another snarl of kudzu? "It's this gully, or that gully," Terry said, pointing out the window at the bottom of a draw. "This property had multiple owners and it won't be easy to get access, much less to figure out where the researchers sampled."

As we toured peach country, I was reminded by the views to the Northwest of the artist/cartographer Mary Ellen Suitt. The views in the distance looked like one of her rich paintings—peach trees and slumbering, recumbent blue ridges. Her scale of dark blues and greens reminded me of one of Terry's mom's paintings I'd seen hanging on his wall, that of Pilot Mountain in the Piedmont of North Carolina. She used a similar palette of rich greens and blues. Suitt's painting looked like it was painted at night, a blue Piedmont midnight with a full moon. The mountains hold so much beauty.

I asked Richter how his upbringing opened up his artistic temperament. "Mothers, all the way," he said, smiling. "Three great mothers in a row. How lucky am I?"

Mothers indeed. This whole story had been about mothers. Though Mama did not paint landscapes she told stories like an artist. She carried forward the story of these gully-haunted Bradleys, who lived their lives peppered through this edge country between

Piedmont and mountains. Their story was alive. It was not hard to extract beauty or story from that landscape. I felt privileged to have had a family that survived, that pushed forward, that even flourished. I felt lucky to have had a storytelling mother who told them to my sister, who told them to me.

Was that what Carl O. Sauer meant when in 1936 he said the Piedmont landscape was a place you needed to take your time with, not to jump in rapidly, and that even when you did jump in, it might not be what it seemed? I'd taken four years to tell this story. Was that long enough or should it take a lifetime?

The last gully site of the day was one of the paleobotanist Donald Whitehead's sample sites, hard against Highway 11, on the south side. Whitehead had studied grains of paleo-pollen from Spartanburg County under a microscope back in the 1950s, located and identified grains, and matched them to plant species both modern and ancient. I loved to think that because of the soil men's work here in the 1930s and Whitehead's work here in the 1950s, this area was "like the La Brea Tar Pits of Piedmont pollen." Terry laughed but cautioned me about such comparisons. I was exercising my curiosity again; one of the ways I had survived my childhood was through my ability to seize on novel facts others might ignore and create a meaningful pattern, to find meaning and satisfaction in that pattern, in spite of what my more mainstream friends might think.

We stopped the truck. By Terry's calculations Whitehead sampled right in the middle of a kudzu field. While Terry triangulated from the shoulder, Richter and I waded into the kudzu thirty yards, like pirates pacing off the distance to buried treasure. When we stopped, Richter dug a hole, what's called a shovel test, to see the soils hidden below the vines. "The world's not made for easy research," he said as he dug. "But I think it's a filled gully." That was enough for Terry and he called us back. Richter shouldered his shovel and we walked through the kudzu to the roadside.

Our gully trip drew to a close. We dropped Richter at his truck and Terry and I continued on. Richter had an hour drive east to do some work at one of Duke's research sites. I wondered who his audio copilot would be that time. Darwin? Humboldt? Dickinson's poetry? Shakespeare's sonnets? Dostoyevsky? We bid Richter safe travels and Terry assured him that he was heading home to work on a talk he'd present soon at a professional meeting they both had a stake in. The name of the research project was a mouthful: "Late Pleistocene, Pre-LGM Colluvial and Organic-Rich Sediments in the Interfluvial Uplands of the Southern Piedmont: A Case Study from South Carolina," and Richter had convinced Terry to add a provocative subtitle, "Fundamentally Rethinking Piedmont Landscapes and Soils." Many of the friends and colleagues who stood on the lips of gullies listening to Terry talk about the history of the Soil Conservation Service work in Spartanburg County back in 2017 became collaborators on this "rethinking" project. Besides Terry and Richter, there were Missy Eppes, Alan Bacon, Sharon Billings, Dan Markewitz, and Alex Cherkinsky. I guess I was a contributor too, though unnamed, as perfect cover for the geopoet.

I was about at the limit of what I could understand of that research anyway. My college geology had served me well, but I was glad that I'd been diverted into deeper thinking about my own family's residence on this landscape, finding words for my emotions. The buried organic deposits that interested me most were my own genes and feelings. I'd call Sandy when I returned and would talk some more about my visitation in Columbus Christopher Bradley's yard. I'd tell her how close I felt to our shared past and how thankful I was she had talked with me about what she had discovered and heard.

Research goes on. Scientists take their best shot. Sometimes the work gets out, and other times it disappears for decades as the work of the soil men of the 1930s did. The onus of responsibility was now on Terry to make the ideas stick this time around, so that they become part and parcel of our shared knowledge of the Piedmont. Would there be enough time? Terry, Dan, and I had all entered into a period of our lives when many friends were dying. Daddy died when he was forty-four. Terry's father was sixty-five. Harrington died at sixty-six. Terry told me Richter had said, reflectively, "Terry,

I've only got three or four big pieces of research left." How many more big stories after this one would I have time to tell?

Before we backtracked to town, I asked Terry for one more favor. I wanted to drive past my nephew Sean's new house he built with his wife out near where Highway 11 intersected with I-26. It's where they had endured their own morality tale about a gully. Sean had discovered that a gully is a wound left on the landscape, and how filling it in was like suturing, how the longer a wound stayed open the longer it took to heal.

"Sometimes the patient isn't what you think it is," I said, thinking of Sean. "Sometimes gullies cover up things. They are mysteries that when solved cause trouble or pain."

We soon passed the one-story contemporary Craftsman home with slate gray siding and tan trim, where Sean and Kim had lived since 2015. The house sat on a knoll, and when the trees across the highway were bare in the winter, they had a nice view of the mountains. Since their first year of marriage living in "Granny's attic" twenty-eight years earlier, Sean and Kim had done well for themselves and their family. Both had good jobs in Spartanburg but had chosen to live in what, for the moment, you could still call country. They'd looked hard to find a prebuilt house in the area, but instead located a reasonable lot and decided to build. The house was set way back from the highway on a sloping, treeless lawn. There were a few clay areas where there were still some runoff issues. Terry pointed out they were "rills soon to be gullies" if not diverted.

When they moved up there, Sean would have been in his late forties, and both their daughters, my great-nieces, would have been already grown. With the birth of McKenzie's daughter Laney, soon after they moved up, we extended our family's interaction with that Piedmont landscape to eleven generations.

Trouble came when the contractor began to excavate for the foundation. "He discovered the lot had a large filled gully through the center of it—brick, dirt, blocks, old appliances and lots of trees." When the contractor discovered the gully, he actually removed some of the trees with a chain saw, but soon could see the extensiveness of the gully fill. I looked over and knew what Terry was thinking. "No jokes here about buried organic deposits, please," I said with my hand upraised.

The contractor then informed Sean of the gully problem and that the county inspector had given them a choice. They could backfill the uncovered gully with gravel or take the much more expensive option of pouring a concrete base layer that the foundation would rest upon. Their tight budget was pushed to the breaking point. Sean went to the man who had sold them the lot, but he denied he had anything to do with the gully fill. He claimed the fill was there from the time when he bought it.

Sean's a smart guy. He did his research. He located past aerial photos in the county GIS system that showed that the lot had been wooded with an open gully through it when the owner acquired it in 2005, and so the man was responsible for the fill. The culprit settled out of court. He agreed to pay part of the extra costs on the concrete base and help Sean and Kim scramble out of the gullying of their dream house project. A gully that nearly did them in.

Mary Ellen Brown Lane among the Books, Christmas
(Sandra Alverson Camby, 1996)

This Book Belongs to Mary Lane

[In February of 1991, twelve years before she died, I gave my mother a hardback journal to write in. She wrote off and on for six years. We found the book in her bedroom on Briarcliff Road.]

Well, everybody's gone home. It's been a pretty good day so far. I went over to Piggly Wiggly, then to Dixie Tire, where Danny inspected my car. I was thinking a lot about the Gulf War and about my nephew Patrick. He's right on the front lines. I hope and pray he comes home. It makes me think about World War II. I knew two boys over there. I can't remember being concerned about it. I really don't think I ever thought about them being in danger. I was young then, fifteen or sixteen. I rested about an hour then washed a load of clothes. So, with a sandwich made and the house all locked up I went to bed early, since I need the sleep.

Goodnight "Sweet Ones."

I will never get much done. Not like I used to. I am really tired now. All I've done is warm up dinner, wash a load of clothes, and press some material. I might cut a suit up. Maybe I'll cut it out tomorrow. Sandy had dinner with me. I sure enjoy her coming by. I have felt real good today, real "feisty." I should ride out to the cloth shop tomorrow, but I don't want to be bothered with the traffic on Highway 29. I don't know what to do about the supplemental insurance. I need it for my medicine. I'm not going to let it worry me tonight.

Goodnight "Dear Ones."

This has been a dreary day. Cloudy and cold, at least cold to me. I've found out I feel pretty good mentally when it's warm and sunny, but today has been like, "blah." I've not got a thing done but warm some dinner and clean the bird cage. Warmed-over pinto beans, chicken and dumplings, broccoli and cabbage, and corn bread. My hip hurts. I hope I don't fall apart before I die.

Goodnight My Family.

I had a great afternoon. Sean and Kim came over and took me to AT&T to turn in my phone. I had been renting it and paying for thirteen years. Sean said I'd paid $1500 for this phone. So I turned it in and bought my own. I paid $32.99 for a pretty phone at K-Mart. I also bought me some panties at Belks. Four pairs. That means I won't have to mend them anymore. I can even throw some away. Sean and Kim are sweet as can be. I love them very much. Oh, I bought some potting soil for the plants in the living room. I hope they will thrive. It's been a beautiful day and much warmer. Got my sandwich, and my gown on. So I guess I'll call it a day. Looks like the war is over.

Goodnight My Hearts.

We sat around the table after Sunday dinner and talked about the old times. When I talk about my growing up years and about the bad times I can remember, I get pretty emotional and stirred up inside. I guess it's a good thing I can't remember all the bad times. We did have some good times too, but I just can't remember anything, so it's just as well. I really enjoy our being together on Sunday. It seems like a kind of magic time. I'm so glad I have lived long enough to see the happiness back in their faces and not see all the fear they used to have when they didn't know if I would be sober or drunk. I wish I could give them back the years I took away from them and from me. I hope and pray I can make up for some of the years.

Goodnight Babies.

I am watching my soap operas today. Sometimes I really get bored with them. You can usually figure out yourself what's going to happen next in the storyline. I really need to go out in the backyard and pick up limbs that have blown down, but it's too cold and the wind is still blowing, so bringing some more down. They say it'll be about seventy degrees on Wednesday. So I'll have to do that then. I've got a pair of pants of Sandy's to shorten but the sun is not shining in the windows enough for me to see to sew. 5:15 p.m. Got myself comfortable with my gown on. Put the bird to bed, so I am ready for bed too when the time comes.

Goodnight My Smart Ones.

My neighbor James came over and told me Mary's brother had died this morning at the hospital in Greenville. He was the one that fell next door when he was drunk and it paralyzed him. I had met him. He was over there a lot. I should cook something tomorrow and take it over there. Maybe some chilled salad.

Goodnight Loved Ones.

I don't think I'll fix any dinner Sunday for the family. My birthday is Tuesday and the only time I would rather go out is my birthday and Mother's Day. Gosh, I'll be sixty-five. I'm watching Regis and Kathy Lee. Oprah will be on at 5:00 p.m. Hope she has a good show today, as sometimes it just stinks. Of course I don't have to watch.

Goodnight My Hearts.

Well, it's been a pretty nice day so far, real sunny but a little cold. To me it's right cold.

I went to eat at Cracker Barrel with Lottie and Boyce. The food is pretty good, but nothing is really good to me except home cooked meals. Golly, I'd hate to have to eat out all the time. I sure hope I stay able to cook until I die.

We rode over some of the town today and some older places we knew of. A lot of the older sections to become nothing but slums. Of course this section I live in now was always one of the better sections to live in but it's going to gradually become a slum in the future. You know that saying, "there goes the neighborhood," when Blacks start moving in seems to always come true. I have real good Black people next door, the best neighbors you can ask for, but as you look on down about three blocks on Briarcliff some of the places Black people are moving into are beginning to look pretty bad.

I guess I shouldn't have written what I did about the Black people. I did have some next-door neighbors that were white, and they were awful. He kept two cars up on blocks in the driveway all the time and he was just so hateful. I was glad to see them leave. Then the Black couple moved in and I thought, "Oh my God," what is the neighborhood going to be like now? They turned out to be the best neighbors I ever had since the duplex was built. The Blacks that have lived on the other side of the street have not been much of neighbors for anyone. Gosh I shouldn't have gotten on that subject of Black-and-white. I believe in live and let live.

Well, I think I'll get on my gown and robe and get comfortable and fix me a bite of supper. I am going to close it up for the day.

So Goodnight My Dears.

I just finished looking through some pinto beans to have for tomorrow. I can't think of anything any better to have on your birthday in addition to beans, corn bread, a dish of cabbage, also a purple onion. Oh yeah, I took the birdcage apart and cleaned it good. I wish that bird wouldn't shit on top of his water container. I wonder how it would work to put a Band-Aid on him. He'd keep a bald ass wouldn't he? Pull his feathers out. Ha ha. I have such a good time laughing. Sometimes I have nobody to laugh with. I guess it's good for me. I can tell you one thing, I don't sit around feeling sorry for myself. I don't get much done as I'd like, but I get the real necessary things done. James helped me pick up the limbs that had blown down. There was a good many of them. We picked up some in the front yard too.

Goodnight My Dear Ones.

Well, it's my birthday, and has not been a very good one. I got sick about 4:00 a.m. this morning vomiting, and I've been sick all day, haven't eaten anything but four crackers. I feel like I got a virus. Was supposed to go eat tonight with Boyce, Lottie, Frankie, and Libby. But I just can't make it. If I'm going out to a nice restaurant I want to be able to eat. Well, I'm going to hang it up this time. Hope I will feel better tomorrow.

Goodnight My Sweets.

I've been watching a Black girl, looks like she's about ten years old, on the sidewalk out front. Boy, was she doing some hot dancing out there for about thirty minutes. She was throwing it up and down and out and over. I've sure never seen anything like that on Briarcliff Road. She really put on a show. There's no telling what will be seen in the summer here.

Goodnight.

The little Black girl did her dance out on the sidewalk again today. I hope she is that happy all the time.

Goodnight My Loves.

I didn't see my little Black girl today. Since it was a pretty day I wonder why?

Goodnight "My Sweets."

Well, Sunday dinner is over, and the table discussion we have every Sunday. I sure enjoy the table talk. We had a good dinner, just a real down home dinner. You can't beat it. Pinto beans, cabbage, squash, macaroni and cheese, pork chops, and cornbread. Also a plain cake with chocolate frosting on top. I enjoyed it. Johnny's only missed one Sunday dinner. He'll be home next Sunday. That means me and Sandy will have leftovers tomorrow. The president is going to greet some troops coming home.

Goodnight My "Dears."

I had to cook dinner today, so I was right busy all morning with that. Then by the time I got to the dishes washed and things put away it was 3 p.m. Then when I came in here and sat down I felt sort of guilty, because there's really a lot more that needs to be done. But I cannot do but so much in a day. Boy, the older you get the slower you get. I never paid any attention to that saying because I just never could see how it could happen. Now I'm sure it happens to everybody.

Goodnight My "Hearts."

I haven't seen the little Black girl for three or four days now. Wonder where she is or if she's just stopped dancing? There were so many feathers in the bottom of the birdcage yesterday when I cleaned it that the bird looks a little skinny today and the feathers are still flying. Maybe Oprah will have a good show.

Goodnight "My Pals."

Sean and Kim are parents today. Kim gave birth to a little girl . . . So beautiful, perfectly formed. Has a little bit of red tinge to her hair. I got to hold her a little and she's so tiny. They named her McKenzie Laurel. That makes me a great-grandmother, but that's all right. I wish I could have the chance to spoil her a little but I know I won't.

Goodnight "Sweethearts."

I saw the little Black girl going down the sidewalk dancing, but she just kept going.

"My Dears."

I have not done anything much today except warm me some dinner. I cut my left hand yesterday on the palm side when I was washing a glass. It just broke in my hand for no reason at all. I've got it all bandaged up. It bleeds when I use it. Oprah just came on. Her show is about money. I need to watch this because I don't have any. But it gives me an idea of where to put it if I had it.

Goodnight My "Wee Ones."

I've been working more on my little word puzzles. This week I figure them out by 10 a.m. every day but today I didn't get it solved until 2 p.m. The answers are in the paper the following day.

When we went to the cloth shop in Gastonia Monday I bought two little cut out bibs for McKenzie and I've been putting them together today. It will be hard to go in a store and not buy something for her. I have not seen the little Black girl for several days now. Maybe she's someplace else for spring break.

Goodnight "Dear Ones."

It's been a long time since I have written anything. I had forgot I even had this journal. It's been a long winter. Spring is finally here. I hope James is getting his garden ready to plant. Maybe I can get some tomato plants to put in for myself. I've not done anything but wash a load of clothes and watch TV. I slept until 8 a.m. this morning. I'm getting to where I sleep later every day. I just finished a book Johnny gave me. I can't read as much as I used to. I guess my eyes need checking again. I'm going to the grocery store in the next few days to find me some Vidalia onions. They'll only be in the store a few weeks. I better get on a gown and call it a day.

Goodnight My Loves!

My ground round has not thawed, so I will have to wait until in the morning to make my meatloaf.

"Sweet-hearts."

Well, it's really poured rain all day and some tornadoes have been spotted. It's just been a rough day. About 12:30 I was watching the news and a clap of lightning and thunder came, and off went my TV. It had not been storming at all because I know to turn off the TV when it does. But it was just kind of freaky. I knew I couldn't get anybody to fix it today or over the weekend, so I called Libby to the rescue. Bless her heart, she came over with her 13-inch TV so I've got something to watch. I know we need the rain but I have to worry also about the basement flooding. It's already rained hard enough for it to flood. If it puts out the pilot light to the water heater, I'll have to call the gas company.

Goodnight "My Sweets."

I called J. C. yesterday to come see about my TV to repair it. He came by this morning and stayed two hours, then said he'll have to take the TV with him. He told me he probably would cost no more than about $45. Then he called about two hours later and said it probably cost close to $85. I just had a feeling that when he took it with me he would call me and tell me it was more. If I could afford it I wouldn't put too much that much money and eight or nine-year-old television. It still seems it was like a freak lightning bolt that came down and hit the TV. You sure better not play TV in the house even when it's cloudy and rainy like that.

Goodnight "My Hearts."

The insurance man came and I sat around talking for a good while. He's a real nice man. Then I worked on cutting out Lyn's prom dress from about 1:30 yesterday until six. It was something to cut out and you have to baste every stitch to do any sewing on it. It's just going to take some time to finish it. Sean brought the baby for Johnny to see. They were on their way to Kim's grandmothers for dinner. My boy Johnny got home yesterday. It was good to have him home. He said he be out of town for two more weekends. It was real sunny and I picked up some more limbs from the front yard. I worked on Lyn's dress all day and I really haven't got that far. I guess it's because I'm a lot slower in everything I do now.

Goodnight "My Family."

Johnny's trying to put up a security light on the front for me. He ran into a little trouble. I do hope he can get it figured out because I feel I need that light out there real bad. I'm cooking some pinto beans for tomorrow. Johnny's going to leave in May and be gone for the summer. He gave me his TV and said he would buy him another in the fall. Got him a new Mazda truck to go on his trip. It sure is pretty. Regis and Kathy Lee just came on so I'll watch.

So Goodnight Munchkins.

I've been working on Lyn's dress all day. It's real hard to work on. That sequin material feels like you're handling a snake. It makes your skin crawl. I'm hoping and praying I do a good job on it for Lyn because I've never made a prom dress before.

So Goodnight My "Sweets."

Sandy called last night and said Johnny's uncle Sidney Lane died yesterday morning. He was eighty-four years old. He had a good long life and he was always a happy-go-lucky one up until his brother George shot him in the face. He couldn't talk much after that. They're all gone now. Sidney started out in Aberdeen picking up garbage at the army camp at all during the war. When John got out of service and he and Sidney opened up a garage. After John and I started dating he opened up the Shell station there on Highway One in Southern Pines.

They really did have a good business there because back then it was the main route to Florida. John ran the station and Sidney a car dealership. I can't remember the make of car he sold. When the company stopped making the car, though, Sidney started selling used cars and always had a good business. When the highway moved over on the other side of them, or rather in back of them, the flow of traffic stopped and that's when John and I opened the upholstery shop in Aberdeen. Then Shell Oil built a new station in the place of the old one across the road Sidney ran it until Sidney sold out to Julian. By then John had died and we left and so I don't know so much about what was going on with Sidney except truck farming and selling used cars. He sure was a go-getter. Always moving around dealing with something. Well, the older ones go, the middle ones just get older, and younger ones are on the way to being middle-aged.

Goodnight "My Family."

I'll be cooking some tomorrow. I have to boil a chicken and cut it up to make chicken casserole for Sandy's dinner. I've got my gown on already and have had a sandwich. So I am just going to sit back and be comfortable.

Goodnight "My Loves."

It's been seven days since I've written anything. Johnny will be disappointed in me. We finally finished Lyn's prom dress. It sure is beautiful. I hope she is proud to wear it. She helped a whole lot making it, as did Sandy. I couldn't have finished it without their help. It's been a pretty day.

So Goodnight.

Well it's really been a very long time, nearly three years. I guess I feel bad about not writing anything. I feel like I've really lost that three years of my life somehow. Really it would take too much writing to put down what's been happening. I've got rid of my car. I really could not afford the insurance and the traffic on Reidville Road is so bad I had got scared to drive out there. I have to depend on Sandy mostly to go to the grocery store. I wish I could take my little grocery cart and walk to Deal's Market for some of my groceries, but when I think of doing that it terrifies me to death.

I did get out with Boyce and Lottie on Friday night to eat and go to Walmart. I've along pretty good in the past having to wait so long for Lottie, and as I write down how it felt I might just sound like I'm losing it. I don't think so. I'll put down how I felt. I understand it myself.

Well, this Friday night they picked me up about 6:45 and we went to Denny's to eat and left there about 7:25. Boyce let us out in front of Walmart. We went in instead of waiting for him. I went to the service desk and Lottie said she was going on and start shopping, and not to wait at the front for Boyce. In the past the three of us would stay together until we got about middle ways of the store, then I would leave them and get what I needed.

I went to get Polident, bathroom tissue, paper towels, dish liquid, seam binding, cigarettes, and an ash tray to replace one I had to return. Then I checked out. I think it was about 8:20. I had my things in a buggy and every time you go and come you have to hand them your receipt to be checked by the woman at the door. I have always gone and sat on one of the benches out front to smoke. I did this Friday night. It began to mist rain so I got my buggy and went back inside to sit on a bench there. When I had done this three times (gone out to smoke) it was 10 p.m. I started to go out a fourth time and I said to the young girl checking the tickets, "I'm beginning to wonder who the hell I come with." They started watching me real strange. She asked me if she could page the person I'd come with. I said no. By then I was feeling strange because I knew who I had come with. But I thought maybe something had happened to Boyce and Lottie. There were hardly any people at the checkout except the people who worked there and they were all watching me.

Finally about 10:25 I saw Lottie at the checkout. They came over and asked me if I saw the people I'd come with. I told her yes and she seemed relieved. I think about ten minutes more and I would have called a cab. I hope I didn't upset Lottie because I told her I'd begun to wonder who in the hell I had come with. She looked at me kinda funny. But we went on to Krispy Kreme and got home about midnight.

Well, Good Morning My "Dear Ones."

Sunday was the first time in years I didn't cook dinner for my family.
[No Closing.]

My seventieth birthday. The past few days I've thought a lot about my childhood, about how I was always being beat and having (or being taught) to fear God. I think you should love and know there is a source, a higher one who created all the beautiful things. I guess people want to say God is love!

I used to think that I never deserved to have everything right for me. I knew I had to go to bed and then get up to get a beating. After all the misery I have a son and a daughter any mother would approve of. And two grandchildren I deserve because I have always loved them so much. And a granddaughter-in-law whom I love also. And what can I say about my two great-granddaughters. My love for them is so great that I know they will make us all real proud.

Be Sweet My Babies.

About two months ago I started reading *Jane Eyre*. I don't know why I had never read it before. I've only got to chapter fifteen. First part of the book was so disturbing I had put it down a lot. The time she spent in the school or orphanage reminded me of school when I was a child. One thing that I remember so well was the school me and Lottie went to at the time. I guess I was nine and Lottie was seven. Anyway Lottie was always the brightest pupil in the school. I was OK but not at the top. Most of the time we had two biscuits with a piece of meat in them called a "streak of lean and the streak of fat." We always got in different lines for different classes in the courtyard and for the principal to make any announcements. It was a rule that said you couldn't eat in line. I suppose that I was a rule breaker. I was hungry and I took out one biscuit from my paper sack and ate some of it, so I was called up to the platform in front of the whole school and paddled real hard on my turned-up palm.

[No Closing.]

I don't really know what to write about but I've had a miserable day. I tried to sew. Too nervous, I've been really depressed all day. I wish Dr. Porter would give me something to get me through the days. I'm so depressed. I know I'm going to have to have something done. I can't sew because of the shaking. Because my legs begin to shake and I look like I'm trying to walk drunk.

[No Closing.]

I've had an awful day today. My legs have give me a lot of trouble. I tried to walk around and do what I could. I had bought four yards of fleece. I figured I could get three covers for lounging in the living room, but of course I cut it wrong. I should leave things alone when I'm this nervous. I know I will mess things up. I've always felt like I was in pretty good health, but since I turned seventy I was just going down. By God I'm going to jump right back to see now that my children don't expect me to ever get sick so I'm going to have to talk to God an awful lot from now on. He and I know I would like more to do in this world and I'm not finished yet. That's what I think he thinks. I can't understand why I feel thirty years old this old body is seventy. It wants to make me feel different. As of now I'm going to bed. Maybe I'll feel better.

"*My Loves.*"

Last entry. Feb 12, 1997.
I've tried to write in my journal often. But I can't. Tonight I just sit here.

[Mama died on the 30th of September 2004.]

John Lane Holding Buried Organic Deposits
(Daniel Richter, 2021)

Airport Gully

If Hoye Eargle and the Soil Conservation Service had a Sistine Chapel science project in the Piedmont, an argument could be made it was the airport gully study. Between 1938 and 1941, with access to Civilian Conservation Corps workers from nearby Greer's Camp Highland, Eargle supervised the augering by hand more than a hundred bore holes, some up to twenty-five feet deep, to sample a system of extensive buried stream valleys and organic deposits exposed in the bottom of a gully system. The core samples were each described in detail and pulled together into elegant cross sections.

The site back then was on Old Highway 101, the road between Woodruff and Greer, gullied farmland, likely the kind Hugh Hammond Bennett had been bent on saving from that devil, soil erosion. In the intervening eighty years the site had become a landscape time capsule of sorts. Greer had gone from mill town surrounded by farms to the epicenter of a global industrial juggernaut. The old farm had grown up in timber, and the land, owned for decades by the Greenville-Spartanburg Airport, served as a buffer to the ever-lengthening runways. Around the pines, hardwoods, gullies, streams, and small lakes, the twenty-first century had closed in like an escaped wisteria vine and strangled the place—jetport to the South, vast BMW plant to the East, and sprawling suburbs of the city of Greer to the West. It took some political wheeling and dealing for a crew of scientists to even get on the property. At first the Airport Commission declined when Terry discovered the location of the site and asked to explore. Then another of the researchers had a family connection and approached them again. The Commission granted permission, but only for two narrow windows, one for reconnaissance and one in the future for follow-up sampling.

I'd been listening for the last few months to the buzz about the site from Terry. He'd had a turn of good luck, and a team had assembled around the project, making it possible to revisit and rework Eargle's old data, gather new data with techniques not available in the 1930s and 1940s, and add some modern interpretation. Hopefully they'd finally publish the work that had been initiated eighty years before.

Many of the people I'd met earlier on the Friends of the Pleistocene field trip were now working on the project. Everyone was excited about the site, and in the weeks preceding my visit, scientists from four different colleges or universities had taken part in the first reconnaissance since Eargle's work was abandoned in the early 1940s soon after the war broke out.

When Terry called to tell me, he had permission to visit the gully at the airport, and I'd thought I'd go out with him as a courtesy. I almost didn't take a notebook. There wasn't a story there I needed. I thought this book was a wrap. This would be just another drive-by report of gully work—found, lost, found, and maybe to be lost again.

But I was drawn deeper and deeper into the gully as Terry talked. Dan Richter had driven over from Union. He stood and ate his breakfast of tuna salad out of a plastic baggy as Terry spread out the paper trail of Eargle's project on the hood of his truck. It was the second time I'd seen Richter since we'd paddled the Enoree together and I'd seen the ghost of Albert Einstein. Where we had paddled was in the same watershed and only a couple of miles away.

We listened as Terry narrated the project using the maps, cross sections, and diagrams of unpublished data that he had recovered from National Archives. "There's a series of transects they established—A, B, C, D, and H." He pointed to a modern photo outlined with a spaghetti of colors demarcating Eargle's 1930s drainages and the transects. "The organic material is here in green. We've been working right in the little place, where there is a little X. They dammed up a network of gullies. Two ponds have water and one does not."

"Farm ponds?" I asked.

"No, these ponds came later. I think they were connected to the airport."

"Have you found a place where the organic matter is visible?"

"Yes. Just barely."

"Can I get down there and put my hands in it?" I asked.

We entered the woods and stood on the lip of the gully head where Hoye Eargle had discovered the organic deposits and the contemporary team had worked a few days earlier on their first recon mission. Our backs were to a beautiful pond, mysterious and hidden by pines, and a large, flat rock outcrop to the North. But here near the top of the drainage was a quarter acre of flat rock. We had earlier stood for fifteen minutes on the amazing outcrop, like nothing, Terry said, he had seen in the area. It was the sort of exposed bedrock you only see in the Piedmont at a knickpoint, a step along a river's profile, like the shoals on the Enoree River where the Soil Conservation Service had installed Einstein's flume. We marveled at the stunted prickly pear cactus, the fruiting mosses, the gray flaky lichen, all surviving in the small patches of soil that had collected in the joints and shallow depressions on the rock's surface. This bedrock was the opposite of the buried organic deposits. This rock was entirely exposed and only the hardiest "organics" hung on like sharecroppers for dear life. As we stood on the outcrop, I noted that maybe the most amazing thing about the spot was that no one had defaced it with graffiti. That was one good outcome of the airport locking the site away for decades.

I stood on the rock and listened. Thousands of people passed in and out of the airport a mile away every day, but we were in the wild. A frog chorus rose from the far shore. Below us a carved grotto the size of a large hall opened. Here researchers had cleaned off a large soil profile on one wall. A thick horizon of gray-blue clay glimmered, and water seeped down the lower portion of the wall. In the days since the wall had been exposed, iron oxide had stained the gray clay rusty in places. "Stay back," Terry warned, nervous as I inched closer for a better view. "It's undercut."

Below us in the gully's wet bottom was the very top layer of what I had wanted to see since Terry began this project years before—the dark, buried organic deposits. There were organic deposits in the

Big Lots and Cox gullies, but they were out of sight. We knew they were in the bottom of the Marshall Tucker Gully, but the deposits had been impossible to see because a house had been dumped on top of them. In the Alverson Gully the kudzu blocked our path, even in winter, when the vines had withered. The deposits were always a step or two below me, always hidden by something.

At the airport gully I stood close to the edge and looked down. I could see the black ribbon of soil. Terry cautioned me, just as he always cautioned his geology students, to stay back from the edge of the road. I could tell he was concerned that I should fall into the gully. The descent to the bottom would make it difficult to haul me out if I slipped. The walls were steep and slippery. I pressed him though. "The buried organics are down there. This is something I have to do. Richter and I can work our way down the gully face. There are handholds cut by the researchers on the last trip. There are saplings to hang onto."

But all three of us were well over sixty years old. I wasn't that little boy in the gully anymore. So, I kept my distance from the edge.

Then Richter nearly tripped over an artifact from Eargle's earlier work that had gone unnoted on their first visit—an iron pipe installed eighty years earlier by CCC workers, protruding two inches out of the top of the soil near the pond. The pipe distracted Terry. He squatted down. He seemed pleased, and it took his attention away from the danger of us falling in. He was happy about the pipe, and soon I was pleased with my imminent encounter with the buried organic deposits. "I thought the pipe was under the lake," Terry said, pointing to a strip of orange flagging tape he'd tied to a sapling near the shore. "With this one located we can now locate the other pipes." He put down his pack and pulled out his modern GPS to get a waypoint for the position of the old marker. He'd forgotten about us.

With Terry busy working, Richter led the pilgrimage. He acted as guide as we descended into the gully. I made a joke about him being Virgil to my Dante. I used Richter's shovel as a crutch on the steep descent.

Gullies seldom heal, but they can be filled. In my case they have been, mostly. Because of our family history I say "mostly" because

I know what our ancestors all knew, that trouble can gather like a storm cloud and the runoff can sweep anyone off his feet.

My people's lives were sometimes gullies but they were more often like grooves in a millstone. They have not been easily eroded. They still populate this county, eleven generations after the first of our forebears set up house along the rivers and streams. It's possible, as Terry often reminds me, to go back even further, to those first hunter-gatherers that roamed over the ridges. They were my true forebears. The ancient cousins who roamed here and possibly crossed this rock were simply the wayward relatives who headed in another direction from camp in Africa and ended up in North America thousands of years and generations later. "These groups were kin based," Terry reminded me once. "When that guy went off in a different direction he didn't go alone. He took his family with him." Like that individual, I was carrying our family with me. I'd gotten them all here.

Ten feet below Terry and the frog-haunted pond, the water tumbled along the floor of the gully. The sky narrowed above us like a slot canyon. I was eye-level with the buried organic deposits. The horizon of clay above looked like blue gum in the gully wall.

Once on the gully floor I sat on a rock with water running over my boots. I'd never laid eyes on the buried organic deposits, though I'd made a big deal out of them. And why so? I needed more than written accounts. I needed contact. What better metaphor for family than something dark and buried, rich and organic? My contact with them wove the Piedmont gullies together with my own family explorations. If you would follow a direct human line back from where I sat to the time represented by the deposits, you'd be one hundred thousand years distant, thousands and thousands of generations into the past. When these deposits were laid down, my people had not even left Africa.

On the gully wall next to us there were shavings where one of the researchers had on the previous day pulled back the slumped soil, exposing the organics. There was something spiritual about the ceremony. Richter reached down and sliced clean a slab of the dark, bluish clay with the pick end of his rock hammer, and then he dug into the brown deposit below with his hands and passed a sample to me. A fresh, rich smell rose from my hands, like the wet bogs of the present day.

I squeezed the dark mass and it compressed, then sprang back. I lifted the handful of black matter to my nose. I smelled the resinous bite of wood buried over one hundred thousand years. I could even taste it if I wanted.

Furrows in Mama's Backyard

By the time Mama died, her earthly body was a farmed-out field, her youthful beauty drained away. She was left living like downpour sludge. We said she was an old seventy-seven. She had not been young for decades, a rag doll sitting in her patched Naugahyde recliner on Briarcliff Road, still smoking like a chimney, a black pitch-pot smoldering on the roadside. Her arteries were slurried with heart-silt, her brown fingers bent at odd arthritic angles.

But Mama was not a relic. We loved her. She was like an outcrop of bedrock for us. The memories of her were harvested ground. She had quit drinking on her own at fifty-five when she had a hemorrhage and the doctor told her, Mary, if you take another drink, you're dead. She claimed she never had another drink. When we visited, she told jokes and we listened. As her mind and body began to fail, she had her hallucinations, but we thought of them as visions. There was a visitation from Wolf Blitzer. There was a mouse in her bathroom as big as the little dead dog Paula she still mourned. Her attention was younger than her body. She noticed everything. She cared about the outside world, especially through the lens of CNN, just could not move within it. Her house was her calcified shell.

After Mama died, the family sometimes met at Sandy's house or up on Highway 11 at Sean and Kim's. That was how we carried on the hard work of keeping her memory alive, often accomplished over food. Mama had been a great southern cook, and my friends liked being invited over for meatloaf and banana pudding.

For years we all went to Mama's house to eat Sunday dinner at 11:30 a.m. We would sit and eat and talk and refigure the family through story. And now it was me who had to tell them, if I tell them at all—the stories of Lon Brown and Mary Ellen and John, my father. The stories want to be out there, to be told—to come to life. One

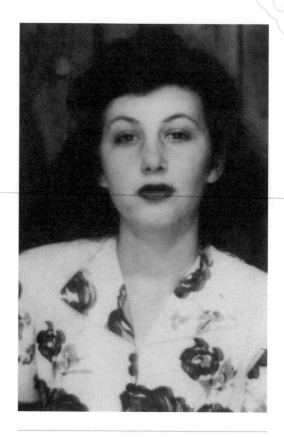

Pageant Photo of Mary Ellen Brown Taken in a Studio, Spartanburg, S.C. (Jack West, 1943)

time, I had gone to buy the collard greens and hog jowl, and, on the phone, Mama had said, "Get it cut nickel thick. You know, the round part." But I had the meat man cut it too thick. Mama tried to make me take it back to the store. "Just bring the whole jowl back," she groused. "I can cut it. What do you think they did before machines?" We both got angry and I realized it was the change, the changing of the guard. If that tradition were to continue, I'd have to learn how to cut hog jowl. We have tried to keep the tradition, though we've given up some things, like hog jowl.

We gathered for holidays almost always as four generations, half our whole line, with the addition of my great-great-niece Laney, who, if she lives to be eighty-four, will peer over into the twenty-second century.

While Mama still lived, she ate BI-LO vegetables and sometimes went downtown to the farmer's market. She liked their tomatoes—homegrown—until once, taking a cue, I plowed the backyard up with a borrowed Rototiller four springs in a row, a pitched-up square of red clay under a thin fuzz of trimmed fescue, the whole plot only four times the size of a double bed. Mama's country-come-to-city tomato patch. Cukes. Okra. Green beans flat and long as her thumb. Yellow crooknecks but no zucchini, which she always called "Yankee squash."

Mama did not come from farms, but she loved fresh vegetables. There were aunts and uncles and they'd visit and come home with produce. Some of them, like Mama's Uncle Will Bradley, worked in the mill, but they farmed too. Mama never said much about farming. All she ever talked about was working in the mill. The Browns, her father's family, came from farming, but she didn't know them until she was in her twenties.

She married into the Lanes. Farming was in their blood. Sandy said Daddy had to have a garden—on Ashe Street in Southern Pines—in the years before he committed suicide. Sandy remembered that before I was born Daddy had a garden up in Maryland where he worked as a telephone lineman. "I remember he planted tomatoes and I laid out in one of the rows and ate green tomatoes until I was sick as a dog."

On Ashe Street, Daddy cultivated the whole sandy backyard using a high-wheel walk-behind. He furrowed, weeded, and plowed. "The hand plow had two handles, a round metal wheel, and a single blade. He plowed it up just like that," Sandy remembered. "He never used a tractor or an animal. Just him. It did what it needed to do."

Mama helped Daddy plant. Daddy told her how to put the okra seeds in the oven and warm them up, "to speed up the sprouts." He harvested what he grew and gave some away. Back when they married, Daddy asked Mama to "cook him up a mess of greens." He said to add some hot pepper, Sandy recalled. Mama asked how much? He said, "Maybe a bole." Mama heard "bowl" and almost killed him then.

Mama canned what was left from that garden I plowed for her every year. Sandy said Mama kept canned goods on a shelf on the back porch—beans, stewed tomatoes, pickled okra. It was an investment in a future that never arrived. When Mama died, we found jars of vegetables unopened.

About four years before Mama died, I went to Wade's, her favorite meat and three restaurant, to get her some "country-style steak," beans, corn, rice, and gravy. I got her a roll and some corn bread, and I took it all over to her. She was so happy to see me. When we sat down to eat, she told me one of her secrets because she knew I would listen, "Johnny, the last two weeks I felt there were presences in the house—spirits."

"Who are they?"

"I don't know but they seem so real to me that one time I turned around in the kitchen and almost offered them some iced tea."

"Are they scary presences?"

"Oh no, they are very comforting. I think they've come to comfort me."

"So, none of them seem familiar enough to name?"

"Well, it could be John."

She seemed comforted by telling me all this.

My present has always been overburdened by the past, but for most folks the recent past encumbers much more directly than deep time. Most people usually can't think more deeply than a couple of generations back. Why should they? Many of my students over the years didn't even know the full name of all four of their grandparents. Not that I put a premium on genealogy, in spite of spending fruitful hours in the presence of Sandy's deep research and truthful answers. Stories are more of a gift than accounting for what we truly know. In the South particularly, stories are the premium. I'd always thought, when I was asked about my people, what was requested was a story, not their names and dates. But stories could hurt, and the scars from them sometimes never healed. To be human is to be wounded.

I dreamed once that a friend recorded hundreds of hours of audio tapes of Mama's stories and gave them to me in a number of decorated boxes for my birthday. I don't know if I ever opened the boxes. The dream ended with the gift. Later, the friend, when asked, said the dream was mine and he couldn't give me an answer.

The relationship I had with Mama was fraught but sacramental. I found a sacred reality in Mama's survival. She never ceased to madden and amaze me. Because Daddy died when I was so young, I have always had a sense of surrogate fathers. My allegiance to Daddy came to me through imagination. The allegiance I have to Mama came though stories. Through Mama I was connected to the daily story of her life and she was connected to mine, which included our deep family story.

What I was talking about was what anthropologists call kinship. It is believed that hunting-gathering people spent much of their intellectual energy recounting the details of kinship. I like to think that meant telling stories. If there was an Einstein back when those small bands walked up the Pacolet River through what is now Spartanburg County, he or she was probably a storyteller. There is wonder both in discovering who you are and how you got there. Look for a blessing. Attend to relationships and bow to the altar of their importance—mother, father, friend, river, gully profile. It is all sacred if we show allegiance and pay attention.

Tailings

A residue of something,

especially ore.

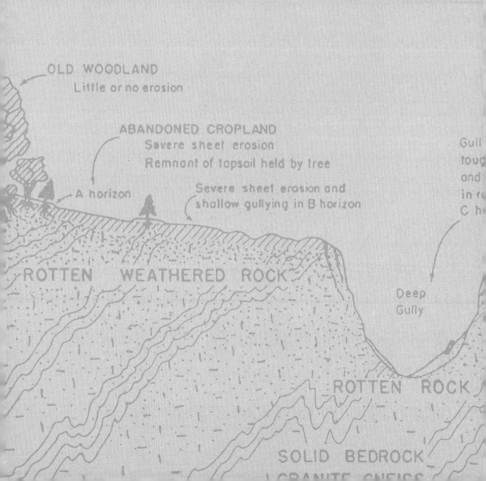

OLD WOODLAND
Little or no erosion

ABANDONED CROPLAND
Severe sheet erosion
Remnant of topsoil held by tree

Severe sheet erosion and
shallow gullying in B horizon

A horizon

Gull
toug
ond
in r
C h

ROTTEN   WEATHERED   ROCK

Deep
Gully

ROTTEN   ROCK

SOLID   BEDROCK

Mary Ellen Brown (Right Top, Sisters, and Dog, Toxaway Mill Village) (Photographer Unknown, 1935)

A Genealogy: Mama's Side

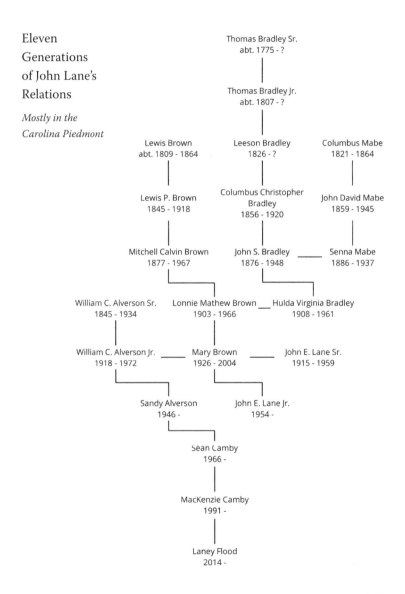

Eleven
Generations
of John Lane's
Relations

*Mostly in the
Carolina Piedmont*

Thomas Bradley Sr.
abt. 1775 - ?

Thomas Bradley Jr.
abt. 1807 - ?

Lewis Brown
abt. 1809 - 1864

Leeson Bradley
1826 - ?

Columbus Mabe
1821 - 1864

Lewis P. Brown
1845 - 1918

Columbus Christopher
Bradley
1856 - 1920

John David Mabe
1859 - 1945

Mitchell Calvin Brown
1877 - 1967

John S. Bradley
1876 - 1948

Senna Mabe
1886 - 1937

William C. Alverson Sr.
1845 - 1934

Lonnie Mathew Brown
1903 - 1966

Hulda Virginia Bradley
1908 - 1961

William C. Alverson Jr.
1918 - 1972

Mary Brown
1926 - 2004

John E. Lane Sr.
1915 - 1959

Sandy Alverson
1946 -

John E. Lane Jr.
1954 -

Sean Camby
1966 -

MacKenzie Camby
1991 -

Laney Flood
2014 -

Acknowledgments

Many thanks to my wife, Betsy Teter, who helped in every way, and to my loyal readers Drew Lanham, David Taylor, Deno Trakas, Venable Vermont, and G. C. Waldrep; to Elizabeth Dodd for an early edit; to Simmons Buntin for asking me to dig deeper; to Terry Ferguson, for the idea; to friends Dan Turner, D. E. Steward, Jim Warren, and Dan Richter for reading early, late, and middle drafts. Thanks to the noble Calzones for listening on a Zoom call to this gully of a story. Thanks to Sandy Camby and Terry Ferguson for providing many of the photographs. Thanks to the dead: my father, mother, and Loren Eisley whose literary ghost still hangs around after all these years to sneak in a cameo. The spirit of poet, paleontologist, and mystic Eisley is in this book. Only in the final draft did I realize that my subtitle ("excavations") bows in the direction of his haunting memoir *All the Strange Hours* (1975).

One of the most important books for me during the process of imagining this project was Paul Sutter's great book, *Let Us Now Praise Famous Gullies*. Thanks to Lisa Bayer, Patrick Allen, Nathaniel Holly, Jon Davies, Erin Kirk, and everyone else at UGA Press once again. The eighth time! You've believed in me for over twenty years. And special thanks to copyeditor David Robertson and to the two anonymous readers at UGA Press who gave very positive and helpful comments on the penultimate draft. I hope they see the book in its present form because the story is better after applying many of their suggestions. May it continue.

And finally, all my love and thanks to my whole family, including my cousin Kitty McChesney. And most of all to my sister Sandy for sticking with me and tracking everything down to the last date and name.

Source Notes

For "Breaking Ground: My Past as a Gully"

"Ansichten der Calzone: Views of the Calhoun Critical Zone Observatory" by Daniel D. Richter and Sharon A. Billings, https://czo-archive .criticalzone.org/images/national/associated-files/Calhoun/Richter _DD2020__Billings_V3_.pdf

A Good Mule Is Hard to Find by Kurt Neeley (Hub City Press, 2009)

For "Big Lots Gully," "Marshall Tucker Gully," and "Cox Gully"

Dance of the Continents by John Harrington (Jeremy Tarcher, 1983)

Discovering Science by John Harrington (Houghton Mifflin, 1981)

"Lecture on Soil Erosion: Its Extent and Meaning and Necessary Measures of Control," address delivered in connection with the South Carolina Teacher-Training Program in Spartanburg, November 4, 1932, from the collection "Speeches of Hugh Hammond Bennett" (National Resources Conservation Service)

Making the Geologic Now edited by Elizabeth Ellsworth and Jamie Kruse (Punctum Books, 2013)

"Man-Induced Soil Erosion on the Southern Piedmont: 1700–1790" by Stanley S. Trimble (Soil and Water Conservation Society, Iowa, 2008)

"Memorial to Dolan Hoye Eargle (1905–1973)" by James Gilluly, Geological Society of America, 1973, https://www.geosociety.org/documents/gsa /memorials/v05/Eargle-DH.pdf

"New Light on the Origins and History of Piedmont Soils and Surfaces" by D. Hoye Eargle, S. C. Academy of Science, 1940

"Oral History interview" conducted with Charles F. S. Sharpe by Anne B. W. Effland, Agricultural and Rural History Section, Economic Research Service, USDA, June 1991, in Alexandria, Va.

"Piedmont Pleistocene Soils of the Spartanburg Area" by D. Hoye Eargle, *Geologic Notes* 21, no. 2 (1973)

Principles of Gully Erosion by H. A. Ireland, C. F. S. Sharpe, and D. H. Eargle, *USDA Technical Bulletin*, no. 633 (1939)

"Report on the Piedmont Field Conference Spartanburg, S.C., April 1–4, 1940," by D. Hoye Eargle (scs Publication)

"Revisiting the Forgotten 1930s and Early 1940s: Piedmont Research of the Soil Conservation Service: Landscape Erosion, Legacy Sediments and Deeply Buried Organic Deposits," a Field Trip Guidebook for the Southeastern Friends of the Pleistocene Conference, February 24–26, 2017, by Terry A. Ferguson, with contributions by Andrew Ivester, Cindy Kolomechuk, and Ben Thomas (available at https://www .digitalcommons.wofford.edu)

Soil Erosion: A National Menace by Hugh Hammond Bennett and William Ridgely Chapline, *USDA Bulletin* (1928)

"Soil Geomorphology Studies in the U.S. Soil Survey Program" by Anne B. W. Effland and William R. Effland (*Agricultural History*, Spring 1992)

"Some Principles of Accelerated Stream and Valley Sedimentation" by S. C. Happ, G. Riddenhouse, and G. C. Dobson, *U.S. Department of Agriculture Technical Bulletin* 695 (1940), reprinted in *Progress in Physical Geography* 32, no. 3 (2008)

Time and the Piedmont by Edward J. Kuenzler (Chapel Hill Press, 2004)

Timefulness: How Thinking Like a Geologist Can Help Save the World by Marcia Bjornerud (Princeton University Press, 2018)

To See a World by John Harrington (C. V. Mosby Company, 1973; reprinted by Holocene, 1994)

For "Deep Family History"

A Broad River Digest by Irene Roach Delpino (Omega Press, 1991)

Reminiscences of Christenberry Lee 1823–1895, appearing in the *Forest City Ledger* during 1895

For "Restoration"

"enr Southeast's 2019 Best Projects: Award of Merit, Renovation/Restoration: The Montgomery Building," *ENR Southeast*, October 23, 2019

A Pictorial History of Spartanburg County by Philip N. Racine (Donning Company, 1980)

Textile Leaders of the South by Marjorie Willis Young (James R. Young, 1963)

For "Rediscovering the Bradleys"

Land & Life by Carl Ortwin Sauer (University of California Press, 1963)
To Pass on a Good Earth: The Life and Work of Carl O. Sauer by Michael Williams, with David Lowenthal and William M. Denevan (University of Virginia Press, 2014)

For "Enoree Flume"

"Apparatus for Sampling Liquid" by Hans Albert Einstein, patent # 2,294,655, U.S. Patent Office, September 1, 1942
Einstein: His Life and Universe by Walter Isaacson (Simon & Schuster, 2007)
"Einstein Made U.S. Citizen," *Greenville News*, September 4, 1943
"Finding Einstein on the Enoree" by R. R. Oborne, *The Outfall* blog, November 2019
"Hans Albert Einstein: Innovation and Compromise in Formulating Sediment Transport by Rivers" by Robert Ettema and Cornelia F. Mutel, *Journal of Hydraulic Engineering*, June 2004
"Hans Albert Einstein in South Carolina" by R. Ettema and C. F. Mutel, paper from Water Resources and Environmental History Sessions at the Environmental and Water Resources Institute Annual Meeting 2004, June 27–July 1, 2004, Salt Lake City, Utah, https://doi.org/10.1061/40738(140)5
"Hydrologic and Hydraulic Research in the Soil Conservation Service" by J. Douglas Helms, Natural Resources Conservation Service, *Historical Insights*, no. 7 (June 2007), https://www.nrcs.usda.gov/sites/default/files/2022-09/stelprdb1044132-hydrologic-hydraulic.pdf
Jim McAllister column, McAllister interviews Jack Nimmons Sr., a ccc worker at the Enoree Flume in the 1930s, *Greenville News*, April 15, 1973
"Klaus Einstein Taken by Death," *Greenville News*, January 6, 1938

For "Alverson Gully"

"A Glimpse of the Divine" by Eric Weiner, *New York Times*, March 9, 2012

"Memorial to Elso Sterrenbert Barghoorn, Jr. 1915–1984" by Warren Meinschein, Geological Society of America, April 1985

"Pollen Analytical Investigations of Pleistocene Deposits from Western North Carolina and South Carolina" by Donald R. Whitehead and Elso S. Barghoorn, *Ecological Monographs* 32, no. 4 (Autumn 1962), https:// www.geosociety.org/GSA/Publications/Books/Memorials/GSA/Pubs /Memorials.aspx

"A Tribute to Don Whitehead 1932–2018" by Jim and Susan Hengeveld, Indiana University, published on the Indiana University College of Arts & Sciences web page, February 2018, https://www.biology.indiana.edu /about/history/faculty-emeriti/memorials/whitehead-don.html

Bio

John Lane is the author of many books of poetry and prose. *Coyote Settles the South* was one of four finalists for the John Burroughs Medal in 2016 and was named by the Burroughs Society one of the year's "Nature Books of Uncommon Merit." As an environmentalist Lane has been named Upstate Forever's "Clean Water Champion" and the South Carolina Wildlife Federation's "Water Conservationist of the Year." In 2014 he was inducted into the South Carolina Academy of Authors. With his wife, Betsy Teter, he was one of the cofounders of Spartanburg's Hub City Writers Project. He is professor emeritus of environmental studies at Wofford College and was founding director of the college's Goodall Environmental Studies Center. There is a gully where he lives on the east side of Spartanburg, and as a retirement project he is filling it with yard debris.